Internet

Timothy J. O'Leary
Linda I. O'Leary

4 5 6 7 8 9 0   BAN BAN   9 0 9 8 7 6

ISBN 0-07-049093-7

Library of Congress Catalog Card Number 95-77789

CONTENTS

The Internet

Every day you see references to the Internet in the newspaper, TV ads, popular soaps and sitcoms, and more. What does all this mean to you? It means that in the future how you learn, do business, shop, or play will be different. Through the Internet you will find amusement, companionship, information—and tremendous opportunity. In the future, not knowing how to use the Internet will be like not knowing how to read today.

Definition of the Internet

What is the **Internet**? It is a network of thousands of computer networks that allows computers to communicate with one another. A **network** is a system that connects two or more computers, allowing sharing of resources. The popular term for the Internet is the "information highway." Like a highway, the Internet connects you to places throughout the world, making available more information than you could read in a lifetime.

In 1993 the Internet connected 45,000 networks. Currently it is estimated that between 2 and 4 million computers in 156 countries are connected to the Internet and that 10 to 30 million people have access to the Internet, 7 to 15 million of them in the United States alone. The Internet is expected to continue growing from about 3.2 million computers today to over 100 million machines on all six continents. By the year 2000, there may be more than 1 million networks connecting 1 billion users, with the majority of these users connecting to the Internet from their homes.

Things You Can Do on the Internet

The uses for the Internet are many and varied, and include the following:

- *Send and receive e-mail.* The largest use of the Internet is to send e-mail (electronic mail) messages between users. **E-mail** allows you to send messages along Internet pathways to users at other computer sites.

■ *Transfer files between computers.* File Transfer Protocol or **FTP** allows you to send (**upload**) or receive (**download**) files between your computer and another computer. The files are made available on the hard drive of computers and are similar to an electronic library of information that can be accessed through the Internet by all users.

■ *Search for information.* The Internet is loaded with information about all imaginable topics. Quickly finding the information you are interested in can be a challenge. Various software programs are available that help you search for information on the Internet. Using one of the search services such as Gopher, Veronica, or WWW (World Wide Web) simplifies this process.

■ *Participate in discussion groups.* **Newsgroups** are databases of messages on a huge number of topics. Users participate in public discussions about the topic by sending e-mail messages to the newsgroup where all participants in the newsgroup can read them. **Mailing lists** are another type of discussion group consisting of a database of people interested in a particular topic. Your e-mail messages are mailed to the addresses of every participant in the mailing list.

Internet Terminology

Download: To copy a file to your computer from another computer over a network.

E-mail: Electronic mail. A message that is sent between users along network channels.

File Transfer Protocol (FTP): A system for transferring files across the Internet.

Internet: A network of thousands of computer networks around the world that allows computers to communicate with one another.

Mailing list: An e-mail discussion group in which messages are sent to each participant.

Network: A system that connects two or more computers.

Newsgroup: A discussion group in which e-mail messages are sent to members.

Upload: To send a file to another computer over a network.

About Labs 1–4

Lab 1   The first Internet lab introduces you to e-mail using the Pine and Eudora e-mail software programs. You will learn how to compose, send, reply, forward, and delete messages. In addition, you will learn how to create a personal address book.

Lab 2   This lab introduces you to two related features of the Internet, mailing lists and newsgroups. You will learn how to subscribe and unsubscribe to a mailing list. The Windows Trumpet newsgroup reader program will be used to learn how to find, read messages in, and communicate with newsgroups.

Labs 3 and 4   In the last two labs, you will use other Windows applications to find information on the Internet. Lab 3 uses the Gopher program to navigate to many locations to access information. You will also learn how to connect directly to another computer and how to use FTP to download files onto your computer. Lab 4 introduces you to the World Wide Web using the Netscape and Yahoo applications.

Before You Begin

The following resources are needed to complete these labs:

- Pine or Eudora e-mail application
- Trumpet newsgroup reader application
- Gopher Winsock application
- Netscape Winsock application

Students need to have an e-mail address and access to computers with a connection to the Internet. In addition, it is helpful if students are already familiar with using Windows applications.

Eudora Setup: Eudora is designed to save the individual's setup configuration to the hard disk of a computer. Your school may need to modify this setup. Lab 1 assumes the following modifications:

- Eudora saves configuration to drive A (change Windows command line to "weudora.exe a:").
- Configuration settings are supplied by the instructor.
- Students need to use the same disk each time they use Eudora. If they do not, they will need to set the configuration again.

WARNING

The Internet is constantly changing. You should be aware that many of the menu selections and instructions in this manual may be slightly different from those at your computer site or at other sites you access while "surfing the net." Most importantly, because things are constantly changing on the Internet, steps and procedures may vary. Be open to trying and searching. You may get lost, but you can always get home.

1   Electronic Mail Using Pine or Eudora

INTRODUCTION

Electronic mail, or e-mail, is the main means of communication between Internet users. It is the backbone of the network and one of the prime reasons for the success of the Internet. Changes in the workplace from central offices to home or on-the-road offices have contributed greatly to e-mail's popularity. E-mail provides a communications pathway to co-workers and customers and allows computer users to exchange information and data files directly with one another.

E-mail is a cost-effective means of communication as businesses become more global. For example, a message that costs $3.12 when sent by telephone, or $1.46 by fax, costs only 23 cents by e-mail. In addition to cost, there is a speed advantage. Messages can be transferred between countries in minutes, and within the United States in seconds. On the other hand, network outages, maintenance, or repair problems may cause a message to be delayed days or even weeks.

In this lab, you will learn how to create, send, and reply to e-mail messages.

About E-Mail

E-mail is based on the concept of **store-and-forward** technology. The message when sent is stored by the originator's computer until the recipient is ready to receive it, at which time the message is forwarded to the recipient.

See the box on the next page for a description of the parts of an e-mail message.

Competencies

After completing this lab, you will know how to:

1. Start your e-mail program.
2. Create and send an e-mail message.
3. Use Help and the spell checker (Pine only).
4. Edit a message.
5. Read and reply to messages.
6. Review sent e-mail.
7. Create an address book or a recipient list.
8. Forward a message.
9. Save a message.
10. Delete a message.
11. Use the global address book (Pine only).
12. Quit your e-mail program.

INTERNET

Parts of an E-Mail Message

Date: Tue, 18 Mar 1997 15:27:39 -0700 (MST)
From: colleen.hayes@asu.edu ———————————— address
To: john.doe@asu.edu

Subject: About e-mail
This is a sample of an e-mail message. ——————————— message

Colleen Hayes 555-0111 Happiness is baseball. ——————— signature line

Addresses

On the Internet, each person has a unique **address** or means of identification. The Internet uses an addressing system called the **Domain Name System** (DNS), which consists of three parts: a unique user name, a domain name (computer name or address), and a domain (class of service code), as shown below.

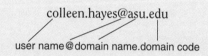

The user name identifies a particular user or group of users at a domain. It is separated from the domain name with the @ "at" symbol. The domain name distinguishes a computer from a group of computers. The domain code identifies the type of use. The most common domains are commercial organizations or educational and research institutions. The domain code is generally a three-letter abbreviation; for example, EDU for education and COM for commercial. Periods, called dots, separate the domain name and code. The number of dots varies depending on how the address is structured for a particular computer.

Attachment

Many e-mail programs also allow you to attach text and non-text files, such as graphic files or spreadsheets, to your e-mail message. If a message has an **attachment**, the name of the attached file appears at the top of the message with the date and address information. The attached file needs to be downloaded to the recipient's computer where it can be opened using the specific software program. The recipient must have the required software program, however, to open the attachment. This sample e-mail message does not have an attachment.

There is a high potential for catching a computer virus through e-mail. This is because attached files may execute a set of commands that can cause damage to your computer system. Protect your computer by using a virus-checker program.

You can create an e-mail message using any word processor. If the message is long and you are paying for on-line time, you may find it useful to create the message off-line and then attach it to your e-mail message.

Signature Line

Many e-mail programs allow you to create a **signature line** that is automatically added to the end of the body of a message. Generally, the signature line includes the sender's full name, postal address, phone number, fax number, and other e-mail addresses. Additionally, the signature may include a quote or some other "signature" that is a means of showing a bit of your personality.

Netiquette

Even though e-mail may appear more like a conversation than a letter (because of the quick speed of response), it is written communication. And like all written communication, the messages can be saved and printed. You can then be made accountable for your words. Therefore, be careful what you say. It is easy to become too informal when using e-mail. Spelling, grammar, and so on may not seem important at the time, but later you may regret your informality.

When communicating using e-mail, you should follow some standard rules of courteous electronic communications as shown below. These rules are commonly referred to as **Netiquette** (net etiquette).

Netiquette

- Never send an e-mail message that you would not want to become public knowledge. Security is low on e-mail communications.

- Never send abusive, threatening, harassing, or bigoted messages. You could be held criminally liable for what you write.

- Because e-mail text is stored in ASCII text codes, you cannot format text to provide emphasis (for example, bolding and underlines). To make up for this, you can surround a word in asterisks in place of italics and place underline characters around a word that you would like underlined.

- DO NOT TYPE YOUR MESSAGES IN ALL UPPERCASE CHARACTERS! This is called **shouting** and is perceived to be very offensive. Use a normal combination of uppercase and lowercase characters. Sometimes all lowercase is perceived as too informal or timid.

- If your e-mail program does not automatically word wrap, keep line length to 60 characters or less so your messages can be comfortably displayed on any type of monitor.

- Ranting and raving—angry flare-ups of e-mail message exchanges— are called **flaming**. Sometimes they are truly angry messages. Others are just meant to spice things up with controversial topics and stances introduced to make the conversation lively.

- Think twice before sending your message: once it is sent, you cannot get it back.

Sometimes written communication is hard to "read." Was the comment a joke or a serious remark? To add tone to e-mail, many people use special pictures of smiling or winking faces called **smileys** or **emoticons**.

> **Look at the picture sideways. The colon is the eyes.**

Smileys

Some examples of smileys and what they mean are:

:-)	Happy
:-(	Sad
;-)	Wink
:-P	Sticking tongue out
:-||	Angry
:-o	Shocked or amazed

Smileys are generally placed following the sentence in question. Other e-mail users enclose remarks in brackets such as <g.> for "grin" and <jk> for "just kidding."

Now that you know what an e-mail message looks like, you will use the Pine or Eudora e-mail program to create your own message.

Follow the instructions in either the Pine or Eudora sections. Pine instructions and marginal notes are shaded in green. Eudora sections and marginal notes are shaded in yellow. All students should complete instructions that are not shaded and read marginal notes that are shaded in tan.

Pine E-Mail ## Starting Pine

The **Pine** program is a menu-based e-mail program that makes it very easy to send and reply to e-mail. Pine stands for "Program for Internet News and E-mail." It was developed by the University of Washington as an easy-to-use alternative to Mail, the Unix-based e-mail program. Pine routes your messages to your recipients via Internet and handles your incoming mail by placing it in your personal storage area.

You can start the Pine program by typing a command at the system prompt or, if your school provides a menu-based access, by selecting a menu option. If your school uses a menu to start the program, your instructor will provide the menu selections you need to make. Write the instructions for starting Pine on your system in the space provided below.

To start Pine from the system prompt: To start Pine on your system:

_____

_____

Type: pine
Press: ⏎Enter

The first time you use Pine, the program may ask if you want to create a separate folder for each month's mail. A **folder** is a named area, similar to a directory, that is used to store e-mail messages. Pine uses a default folder named Sentmail to store copies of messages you send. Pine also maintains other folders that are used to store other categories of messages, such as incoming messages

If the prompt to create monthly folders is not displayed, the Main menu appears. Skip to Figure 1-1.

If the prompt to create monthly folders appears, responding Yes will create a monthly folder and name it using the month name, such as "sentmail-oct-1996." For each subsequent month a new folder is created for that month's mail. If you choose No, Pine uses the default mail folder named Sentmail. If your school permits you to create monthly folders, to respond Yes to the prompt,

Type: Y (Yes)

Otherwise,

Type: N (No)

Your screen should be similar to Figure 1-1.

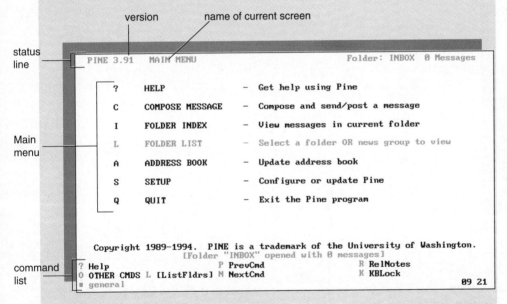

FIGURE 1-1

If you are using PC-Pine, your screen will look more like a Windows application. However, the menus and commands are the same.

The Main menu screen appears. The top line of the screen is the **status line**. It currently displays the version of Pine you are using and information about the program status. The information in the status line changes as you perform different tasks using Pine.

The main area of the screen displays a menu of seven options. These are the Main menu options that when selected allow you to access the main features of Pine. The bottom two lines of the screen display a list of commands. The commands in this list vary with the different features you are using.

INTERNET

Starting Eudora

The **Eudora** program is a Windows-based e-mail program that makes it very easy to send and reply to e-mail. Eudora Software was developed by QUALCOMM Incorporated. Eudora routes your messages to your recipients via Internet and handles your incoming mail by placing it in your personal mail box.

Load Windows. Open the program group containing the Eudora program icon.

Click: Eudora

Your screen should be similar to Figure 1-2.

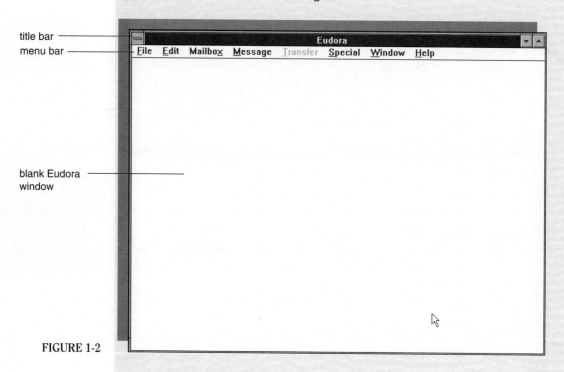

title bar

menu bar

blank Eudora
window

FIGURE 1-2

Because Eudora is a Windows program, it includes all the common Windows elements such as a title bar, control-menu box, menu bar, and maximize and minimize buttons. The title bar currently displays the program name. The large empty area below the menu bar is where the windows you open in Eudora will appear.

When you start Eudora for the first time, you must set the configuration to include your personal information. To do this, the Configuration command on the Special menu is used. As in other Windows applications, you select from the menu bar by clicking on the item or command with the mouse. If you are using the keyboard, you must activate the menu bar by pressing Alt. Then a menu item or command can be chosen by typing the underlined letter or by moving the highlight to the command and pressing ←Enter.

To enter your configuration settings,

Choose: S̲pecial>C̲onfiguration

The Configuration dialog box is used to enter your personal information. Enter the information in the Configuration dialog box as indicated by your instructor.
   To close the dialog box and update the configuration,

Your instructor will provide you with the information to enter in these boxes.

Choose: OK

Skip to the section "Creating a Message" on page IN15.

Pine E-Mail **Using Help (Pine Only)**

The first Main menu option is Help. Notice that is also the first command in the command list. Help appears as a menu option only in the Main menu. However, it is generally available as an option in the command list. Selecting this option displays Help information on how to use Pine. Pine help is **context sensitive.** This means the Help information that is displayed is directly related to the screen you are currently viewing.
   Menu options are selected by typing the character to the left of the option name, in this case, ?. To display Help information about the Main menu screen,

Type: ? (Help)

Your screen should be similar to Figure 1-3.

current screen   line location

FIGURE 1-3

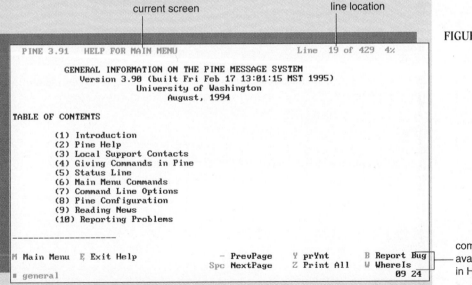

commands available in Help

The status line indicates that you are viewing Help for the Main menu. It also displays your line location (19 of 429) in the Help text file. A table of contents listing of the topics presented in this Help file is displayed. Because you were viewing the

Main menu screen, Help includes information about the Main menu screen as well as general overview information.

Notice that the command list has changed to reflect the commands you can use to navigate within Help. To read the next page of Help information,

Press: Spacebar

Your screen should be similar to Figure 1-4.

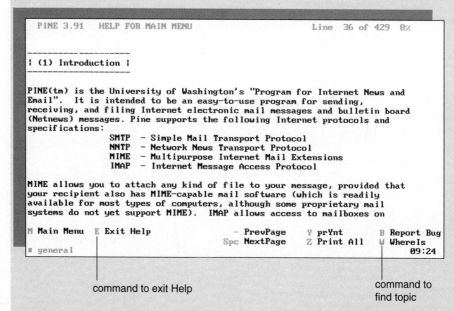

```
  PINE 3.91   HELP FOR MAIN MENU                    Line  36 of 429  8%


  ------------ ----------
  ¦ (1) Introduction ¦
  ----------------------

  PINE(tm) is the University of Washington's "Program for Internet News and
  Email".  It is intended to be an easy-to-use program for sending,
  receiving, and filing Internet electronic mail messages and bulletin board
  (Netnews) messages. Pine supports the following Internet protocols and
  specifications:
                 SMTP  - Simple Mail Transport Protocol
                 NNTP  - Network News Transport Protocol
                 MIME  - Multipurpose Internet Mail Extensions
                 IMAP  - Internet Message Access Protocol

  MIME allows you to attach any kind of file to your message, provided that
  your recipient also has MIME-capable mail software (which is readily
  available for most types of computers, although some proprietary mail
  systems do not yet support MIME).   IMAP allows access to mailboxes on

  M Main Menu  E Exit Help            -  PrevPage    Y prYnt      B Report Bug
                                     Spc NextPage    Z Print All  W WhereIs
  ? general                                                            09:24
```

FIGURE 1-4

command to exit Help   command to
                                                        find topic

Read the information on this screen.

You can also use the ↓ key to scroll the text line by line on the screen. To scroll to the end of the next paragraph,

Press: ↓ (7 times)

You can also move to a desired topic within Help by using the WhereIs command in the command list. To see Help information about the status line,

Type: W (WhereIs)

A prompt appears at the bottom of the screen asking you to enter a word to search for. The blinking box is the **cursor**. It shows where each character you type will appear.

Type: status line
Press: ←Enter

Help now displays information on the status line. Notice that the status line now indicates that you are viewing line 171 of 429 of Help.

To exit Help and return to the screen you were last viewing,

Type: E (Exit Help)

You can always get to Help by pressing ? or $\boxed{\text{Ctrl}}$ + G (Get Help), depending upon where you are in the Pine program.

Creating a Message

Pine E-Mail

From the Main menu, the Compose Message command is used to create and send a message.

Type: C (Compose Message)

Your screen should be similar to Figure 1-5.

cursor   name of current screen

FIGURE 1-5

header lines

body

commands available in Compose Message

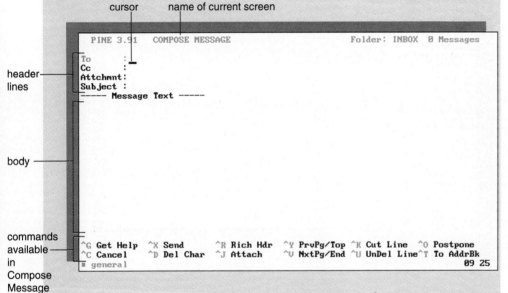

The Compose Message screen is displayed. The status line displays the screen name. This screen is used to write, edit, and send e-mail messages. The command list now displays the commands that are available when the cursor is positioned in the header of the Compose Message screen.

> Command shortcut keys
> appear below the menu
> command preceded with a ➤.

> Keys separated with a + mean
> to hold down the first key while
> pressing the second key.

Eudora

To create a new message, the New Message command on the Message menu
is used.

Choose: Message>New Message
    ➤   [Ctrl] + N

Your screen should be similar to Figure 1-6.

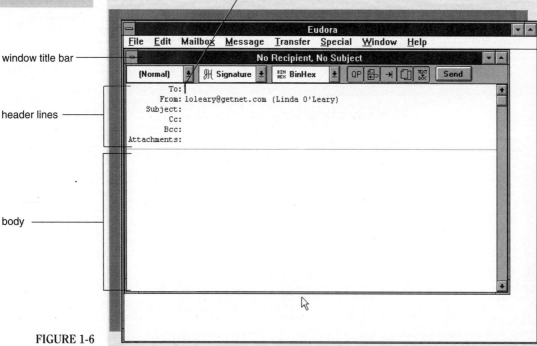

insertion point

window title bar

header lines

body

FIGURE 1-6

The new message window is used to write, edit, and send e-mail messages.
The window title bar displays "No Recipient, No Sender," because you have
not yet started a message. The buttons below the title bar are shortcuts for
commonly used menu options while creating a message.

An e-mail message consists of two parts, the header and the body. The **header**
consists of the lines at the top of the screen containing the address information. The
body, the large blank area in the center of the screen, displays the text of the
message.

The first header line is used to enter the address of the recipient of the message. If you are using Eudora, the second line displays your name and e-mail address. The Cc line is used if you want to send a carbon copy of your message to
another person at their address. The Attachments line is used to specify a file to
attach to your message. The Subject line is used to enter a brief description of the
contents of the message.

You will practice creating an e-mail message by composing and sending a
message to yourself.

Every message must include addressing information so the program knows where to send the message. Read the information in the box on How to Find Addresses.

How to Find Addresses

The best way to find an address is to ask the computer user directly, by telephone or through mutual friends. You can also use one of the following utility programs to locate addresses.

FINGER   Available on Unix machines to provide user names of individuals on a local system. If a user has added their e-mail address, this is a good source. Finger can be used to find information on a specific user or to find out which users are currently using the network.

WHOIS   Provides names, titles, or addresses for about 700,000 Internet users. This is not a standard part of many operating systems and must be installed in many cases. It is also included in many Internet software packages.

NETFIND   Accesses many databases and checks the information on the user's last use of the network and the last computer from which that user read mail.

CSO Servers   Many system administrators make users' addresses available through the Gopher or Netscape applications. The addresses are compiled into lists by geographic or corporate locations. If you know the person's name or where they work, these lists are a good source of addresses.

The address is entered in the To line. The cursor in Pine, or the insertion point in Eudora, is waiting for you to enter the address. Your school will provide you with an e-mail address. Write your e-mail address in the space below:

_____

To enter the address,

Type: your e-mail address
Press: Tab ⇥

If necessary, move to the Subject line.

The subject should be a short, descriptive phrase about the contents of the message. As much of the subject line as space allows will be displayed on the recipient's incoming message. To enter a subject for your message,

Type: A new message on e-mail

You will leave the remaining header lines blank.

Move to the message area.

> Refer to the box on page IN8 to review the parts of an e-mail address.

> Pine: You can also press ↓ or ↵Enter to complete a line and move to the next line.

> You can send a message to multiple recipients by separating the addresses with a comma.

> Eudora: Use the Tab ⇥ key to move to the message area.

> Pine: Use the ↓ key to move to the message area.

INTERNET

The cursor appears at the left margin in the large area below the line. This is where you enter the body of the message.

The e-mail program you are using contains a built-in text editor that helps you easily enter and edit your messages. Like a word processor, it automatically wraps the text to the beginning of the next line when the text reaches the right edge of the screen. Therefore, you do not need to press ←Enter at the end of each line.

The directional arrow keys along with the following navigation keys can be used to move the cursor.

Pine: The Message Text line is now highlighted, indicating it is the area that is selected on the screen.

Moving the Cursor

Pine	Eudora	Action
Ctrl + A	Home	Beginning of line
Ctrl + E	End	End of line
Ctrl + @		Next word
Ctrl + Y	Page Up	Previous page
Ctrl + V	Page Down	Next page
	Ctrl + Home	Beginning of message
	Ctrl + End	End of message

Eudora: The mouse can also be used to move the insertion point. Move to the location and click to reposition the insertion point.

To enter the message,

This message includes an intentional spelling error.

Type: Thiss is the body of the message. When you type, the text automatically wraps to the beginning of the next line when it reaches the right margin. This is called word wrap.

Your screen should be similar to Figure 1-7A (or Figure 1-7B for Eudora).

FIGURE 1-7A

e-mail address   subject of message

text of body of message

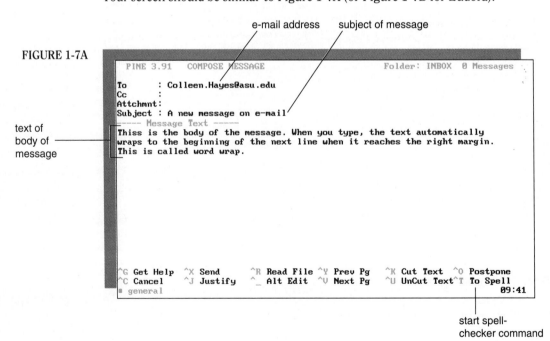

start spell-checker command

e-mail address   subject of message

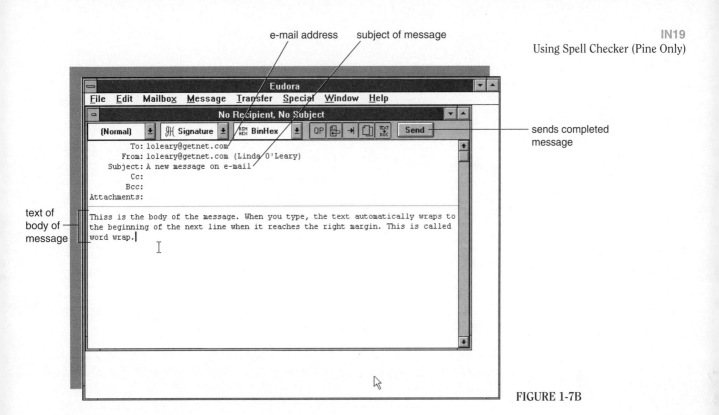

text of
body of
message

sends completed
message

FIGURE 1-7B

Using Spell Checker (Pine Only)

Pine E-Mail

The command list now displays commands that are available when the cursor is positioned in the body of the Compose Message screen. It now includes the command ^T To Spell, which starts the **spell checker**. The spell checker program checks each word in the message against a dictionary of words. If it cannot find a match, it highlights the word so you can edit it if needed. To spell-check this message from the beginning, move the cursor to the beginning of the message.

Press: Ctrl + T (To Spell)

Pine: The ^ character before the letter represents the Ctrl key.

Keys separated with a + mean to hold down the first key while pressing the second key.

INTERNET

Your screen should be similar to Figure 1-8.

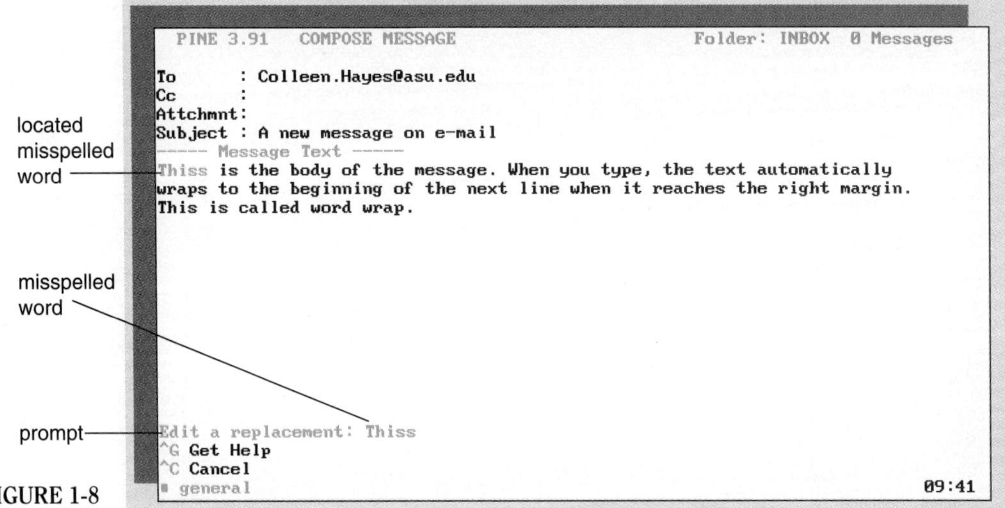

located
misspelled
word

misspelled
word

prompt

FIGURE 1-8

```
PINE 3.91     COMPOSE MESSAGE                    Folder: INBOX   0 Messages

To      : Colleen.Hayes@asu.edu
Cc      :
Attchmnt:
Subject : A new message on e-mail
------ Message Text ------
Thiss is the body of the message. When you type, the text automatically
wraps to the beginning of the next line when it reaches the right margin.
This is called word wrap.






Edit a replacement: Thiss
^G Get Help
^C Cancel
# general                                                          09:41
```

The spell checker has located the misspelled word "Thiss" and highlighted it in the message. The prompt "Edit a replacement" followed by the misspelled word appears at the bottom of the message text area. Now the command list displays only two options, Get Help and Cancel. To get Help information on what you should do next,

Press: Ctrl + G (Get Help)

Help information directly related to the task you were performing, in this case using the spell checker, is displayed.

Read the information on how the spell checker works. To close Help,

Type: E (Exit Help)

You are returned to the Compose Message screen. To correct the spelling, the word following the prompt must be edited. To remove the extra "s,"

Press: Backspace

To accept the replacement word,

Press: ←Enter

The spell checker replaces the misspelled word in the message with the correct spelling and continues to check the message for other errors.

Correct the spelling of any other words the program locates.

When no more errors are located, the message "Done checking spelling" is displayed above the command list.

Editing a Message

Before sending the message, you would like to edit it by adding a new sentence. The following editing features can be used.

Editing Features		
Pine	**Eudora**	**Action**
End		Reformats edited paragraph
Ctrl + K		Deletes current line
Ctrl + U		Undeletes last deleted line
Delete	Delete	Deletes current character
Backspace	Backspace	Deletes character to left
	Ctrl + Z	Undoes last action
	Ctrl + X	Cuts selected text
	Ctrl + C	Copies selected text
	Ctrl + V	Pastes text
	Ctrl + A	Selects all

Move the cursor or insertion point to the end of the *first* sentence.

To add a new sentence to the message,

Type: **Do not worry if you make typing errors. They can easily be fixed using many different editing features.**

Reread the message and use the editing features to correct any typing mistakes.

> Refer to the box on page IN18 on how to move the cursor.

> Pine: Press Ctrl + J or End to reformat the paragraph.

Sending a Message

Now that your message is complete, you can send it.

Pine E-Mail

The ^X (Send) command shown in the command list is used to send messages.

Press: Ctrl + X (Send)

The prompt "Send message?" appears above the command list. To confirm that you want to send the message,

Type: Y (Yes)

Pine displays a message indicating that it is sending mail and copying it to the Sentmail folder. After the message is sent, you are returned to the Main menu.

In a few moments, Pine will display the message "[New Mail! From<Student address> with regard to A new message on e-mail]" to notify you that you have received a new message. This message can be received at any time while you are using Pine. The status line will also indicate that you have a message.

If your e-mail program is running in the background while you are using other programs, your computer beeps to alert you of a new message.

The ❏Send❏ button is used to send the message. To send the message,

Click: ❏Send❏

Note: If your window displays a ❏Queue❏ button instead of a ❏Send❏ button, click the ❏Queue❏ button to place the message in a waiting list of messages to be sent, then choose Send Queued Messages from the File menu to send the message.

The Send Immediately option on the Message menu or the shortcut ⌃Ctrl⌄ + E can also be used to send a message.

Eudora displays message boxes as the message is being sent.

Checking Incoming Mail

When Pine sends a message, it automatically keeps a copy of the message for you in the Sentmail folder. Incoming messages are stored in another folder named Inbox. The Folder List command is used to open folders so you can view their contents.

Type: L (Folder List)

Your screen should be similar to Figure 1-9.

FIGURE 1-9

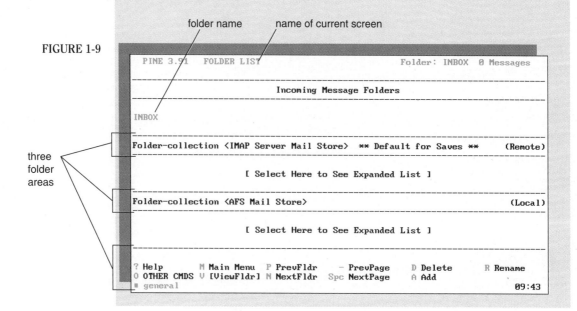

Depending upon your system's setup, your Folder List screen may be similar to that shown in Figure 1-9, where the screen is divided into folder areas: Incoming Message Folders and two (or more) folder collection areas. On other systems, the Folder List screen may simply show a single list of folders beginning with Inbox, then Sentmail and Saved-messages, with other folder names following in alphabetical order.

To view mail you have received, you need to open the Inbox folder. Generally, the word "INBOX" is highlighted by default. This indicates that it is the current option and can be selected simply by pressing ⏎Enter.

Press: ⏎Enter

If it is not highlighted, use the directional keys to move the highlight to it.

Your screen should be similar to Figure 1-10.

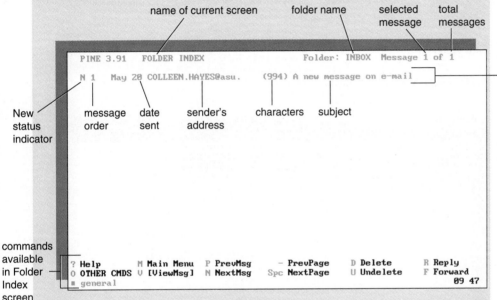

name of current screen   folder name   selected message   total messages

FIGURE 1-10

```
PINE 3.91   FOLDER INDEX              Folder: INBOX  Message 1 of 1

N 1  May 20 COLLEEN.HAYES@asu.  (994) A new message on e-mail
```

message header line

New status indicator   message order   date sent   sender's address   characters   subject

```
? Help        M Main Menu  P PrevMsg    - PrevPage   D Delete     R Reply
O OTHER CMDS  V [ViewMsg]  N NextMsg  Spc NextPage   U Undelete   F Forward
■ general                                                          09 47
```

commands available in Folder Index screen

The status line indicates you are now viewing the Folder Index screen. It also displays the folder name and the number of the selected message out of the total messages. Below this information is a message header line of summary information for each message in your Inbox folder. The message you just sent should appear as the only message (or last message, if you have received others) in the list. It should also be highlighted, indicating it is the selected message.

The letter N at the beginning of the message header line is a **status indicator**. It means the message is new since the last time you used Pine. Other letters that may appear are U for Unread, which indicates the message was not read the last time you used Pine, or D for Delete, indicating the message is marked for deletion. If a blank appears, this indicates the message was read.

The next entry on the message header line is a number. This shows the order in which the message was received. The number is followed by the date the message was sent, the sender's address, the size of the message in characters, and as much of the subject text line as can fit.

If you have a lot of messages in your Inbox, Pine displays the message headers one page at a time. The command list displays the commands you can use to navigate and work in the Folder Index screen.

If you have used Pine before this, you may have more than one message.

INTERNET

When Eudora sends a message, it automatically keeps a copy of the message for you in a mailbox named Out. A **mailbox** is an area on your disk that is used to store messages. Incoming messages are stored in another mailbox named In. The first time you load Eudora for the day, you need to check for incoming mail. To check for mail and have it displayed in your In mailbox,

Choose: File>Check Mail
➤   Ctrl + M

Eudora displays an Enter Password dialog box. Enter your password and choose OK.

Eudora displays a message indicating that you have new mail. To close the New Mail message box,

Choose: OK

Your screen should be similar to Figure 1-11.

> Your instructor will provide you with your password.

FIGURE 1-11

In mailbox with new messages ————

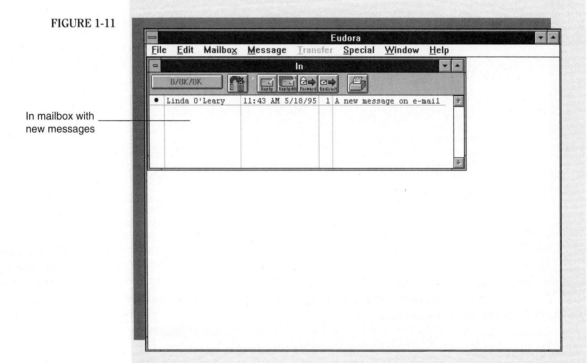

The In mailbox is displayed. The window displays shortcut buttons for commonly used menu options that are available when you use the In window. You will use some of these buttons later in the lab.

Reading Mail

To view the message, you first select or highlight the line with the message information. Then, to view or read the current message, press ←Enter.

If necessary, highlight the message line of the message you received.

Press: ←Enter

Your screen should be similar to Figure 1-12A (or Figure 1-12B for Eudora).

Pine: You can also use the V [ViewMsg] command to view a message.

Pine: You can use the J (Jump) command followed by a message number to move to a specific message. (On some setups, you can simply type the number.)

date and time message was sent   name of current screen   sender's address   recipient's address

header —

body of message —

commands available in Message Text screen —

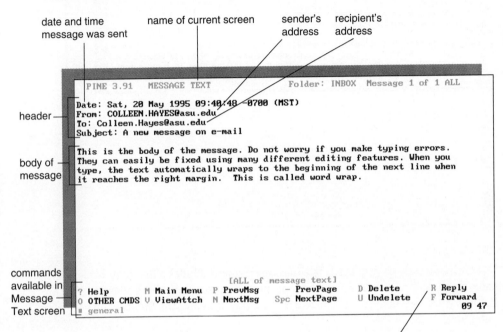

```
  PINE 3.91    MESSAGE TEXT              Folder: INBOX  Message 1 of 1 ALL

Date: Sat, 20 May 1995 09:40:48 -0700 (MST)
From: COLLEEN.HAYES@asu.edu
To: Colleen.Hayes@asu.edu
Subject: A new message on e-mail

This is the body of the message. Do not worry if you make typing errors.
They can easily be fixed using many different editing features. When you
type, the text automatically wraps to the beginning of the next line when
it reaches the right margin.  This is called word wrap.




                        [ALL of message text]
? Help        M Main Menu  P PrevMsg    - PrevPage    D Delete      R Reply
O OTHER CMDS  V ViewAttch  N NextMsg  Spc NextPage    U Undelete    F Forward
■ general                                                            09 47
```

FIGURE 1-12A

command to reply to the message

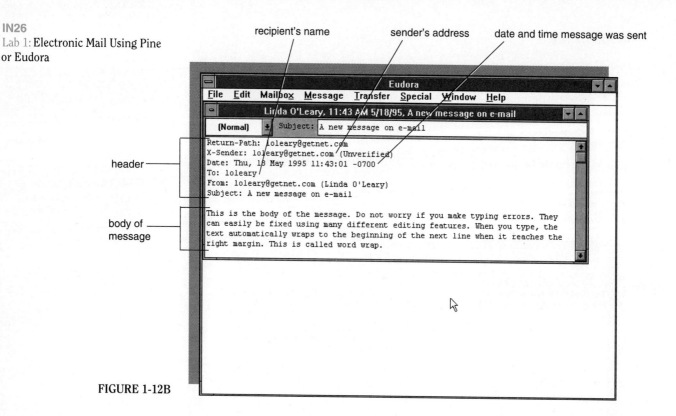

FIGURE 1-12B

The entire message is displayed. The message header includes a line that displays the date the message was sent, the address of the sender, the recipient's address, and the Subject line. The body of the message is displayed below the subject, just as you entered it.

When you are finished reading a message, you can either reply to it, forward it, file it, delete it, or just leave it.

Replying to E-Mail

Many times after reading a message, you will want to reply to the message. When the message header is highlighted or you are viewing the message, it is not necessary to type in the recipient's address and subject information. The Reply command will automatically enter the sender's address as the recipient for you.

To reply to your message (you should still be viewing it),

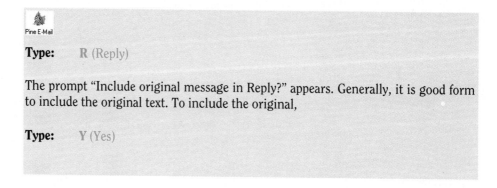

Pine E-Mail

Type: R (Reply)

The prompt "Include original message in Reply?" appears. Generally, it is good form to include the original text. To include the original,

Type: Y (Yes)

If the message "Reply to all recipients" is displayed,

Type: N (No)

Your screen should be similar to Figure 1-13.

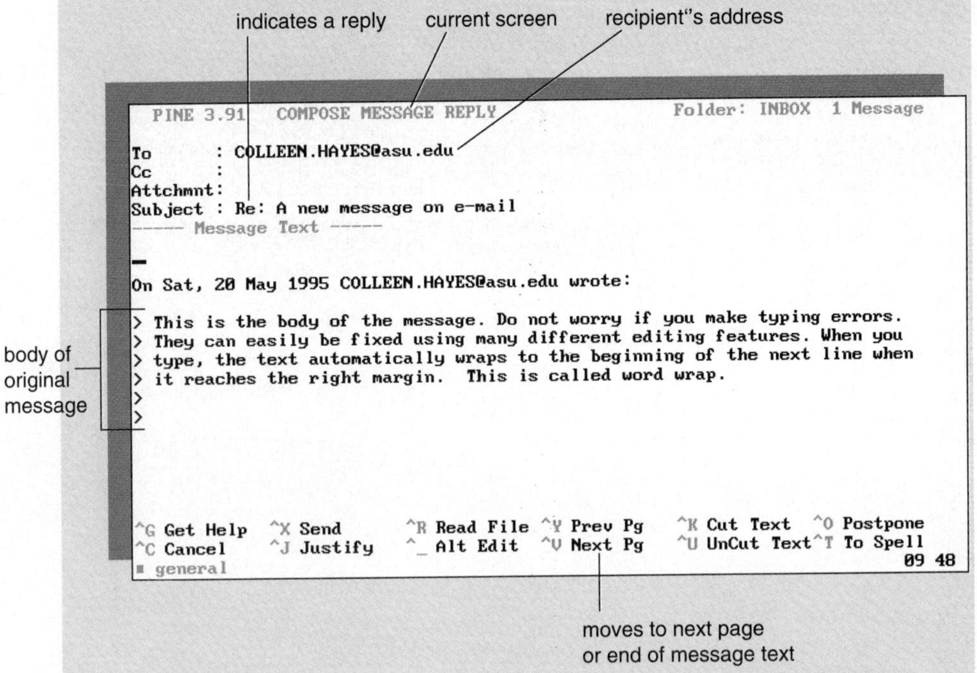

indicates a reply   current screen   recipient''s address

FIGURE 1-13

```
     PINE 3.91    COMPOSE MESSAGE REPLY              Folder: INBOX  1 Message

  To      : COLLEEN.HAYES@asu.edu
  Cc      :
  Attchmnt:
  Subject : Re: A new message on e-mail
  ------ Message Text -----

  _
  On Sat, 20 May 1995 COLLEEN.HAYES@asu.edu wrote:

  > This is the body of the message. Do not worry if you make typing errors.
  > They can easily be fixed using many different editing features. When you
  > type, the text automatically wraps to the beginning of the next line when
  > it reaches the right margin.  This is called word wrap.
  >
  >




  ^G Get Help   ^X Send      ^R Read File ^Y Prev Pg   ^K Cut Text  ^O Postpone
  ^C Cancel     ^J Justify   ^_ Alt Edit  ^V Next Pg   ^U UnCut Text^T To Spell
  ■ general                                                           09 48
```

body of
original
message

moves to next page
or end of message text

INTERNET

The Message>Reply command or Ctrl + R can be used to reply to a message from a mailbox.

Click: 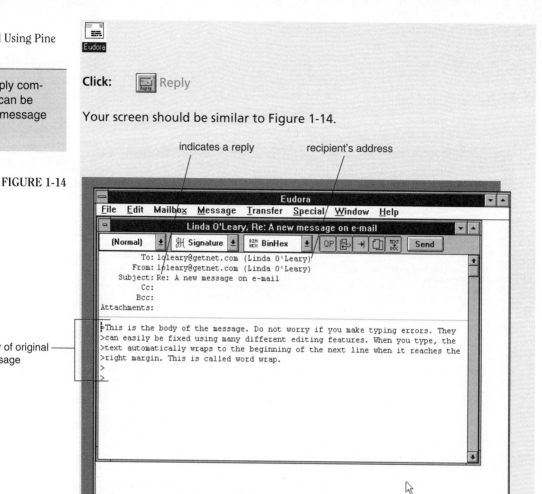 Reply

Your screen should be similar to Figure 1-14.

FIGURE 1-14

indicates a reply   recipient's address

body of original message

Pine: A brief sentence that includes the date and sender's name introduces the original text.

Pine: To quickly move to the end of the message, press Ctrl + V (Next Pg).

Eudora: To quickly move to the end of the message, press Ctrl + End.

The address of the recipient automatically appears in the To text line, and the original subject text is entered following Re: in the Subject line. The text from the original message is automatically copied into the body of the new message with > characters beginning each line. You can edit the original message and/or add your own new message as your reply, just as you did when composing a new message. If the original message is long and you are replying to only part of the message, you can edit the original message to include only the text you are replying to before sending the reply.

A cursor or insertion point appears at the beginning of the message text area. Generally, when including the original message with a reply, it is better to type the new message below the included text. Move the cursor to the end of the message.

On a new blank line,

Type: This is a reply to my original message.

Send the reply. After the message is sent, the original message is displayed again.

Pine E-Mail

Next you would like to return to the Inbox Index Folder screen. Currently, there are no commands in the command list that indicate this is possible. However, the O (Other Cmds) command will display a second list of available commands.

Type: O (Other Cmds)

The I (Index) command will return you to the Folder Index screen, and the L (ListFldrs) command will return you to the Folder List screen. To redisplay the index,

Type: I (Index)

While you are doing this, a new mail message may be displayed, indicating that your reply has been received in the Inbox.

Your screen should be similar to Figure 1-15.

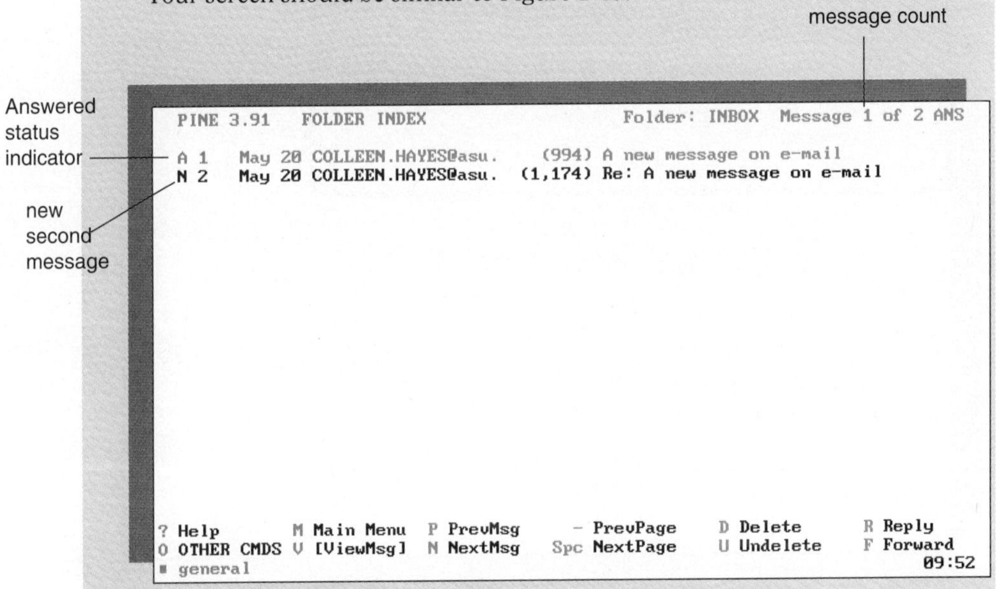

message count

FIGURE 1-15

Answered status indicator

new second message

```
  PINE 3.91    FOLDER INDEX                Folder: INBOX  Message 1 of 2 ANS

  A 1    May 20 COLLEEN.HAYES@asu.    (994) A new message on e-mail
  N 2    May 20 COLLEEN.HAYES@asu.  (1,174) Re: A new message on e-mail












? Help        M Main Menu  P PrevMsg     - PrevPage   D Delete     R Reply
O OTHER CMDS  V [ViewMsg]  N NextMsg   Spc NextPage   U Undelete   F Forward
■ general                                                          09:52
```

The Inbox Folder Index screen appears again. The status line indicates that there are two messages, and the new message header is displayed below your first message. The new message is preceded with an N indicator, indicating that it has not been read, while the first message displays an A indicator, which means that it has been answered.

View your new message.

INTERNET

Next you would like to return to the In window. To close the message window,

You can also double-click on
the message window's control-
menu box.

Choose: File>Close
➢   Ctrl + W

The In window is displayed again.
Check for new mail and close the New Mail message box when the message is received.
Your screen should be similar to Figure 1-16.

FIGURE 1-16

two messages ——
message replied to ——
new second message ——

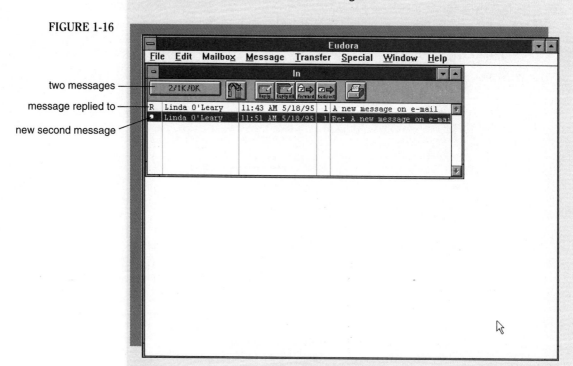

The In mailbox now displays two messages. The new message header is displayed below your first message. Messages are displayed in the order in which they are received. The new message is preceded with a •, indicating that it has not been read, while the first message displays an R, which means it has been replied to.
View your new message.

Reviewing Sent E-Mail

Pine E-Mail

Sometimes you may want to review all the messages you have sent. To do this, you need to return to the Folder List screen and open the Sentmail folder, which contains copies of all your messages. To display the Folder List screen,

Type: L (ListFldrs)

The folder you want to open is Sentmail.

If your setup is a simple configuration, the Sentmail folder should be displayed in the folder list. If this is the case, skip to Figure 1-17.

If your folder list is divided into collections, you will first need to move to the appropriate collection area and display the folders in the collection by selecting "[Select Here to See Expanded List]." If this is your system setup,

Select: [Select Here to See Expanded List]

The names of the folders in that collection are listed.

Your screen should be similar to Figure 1-17.

> You do not need to display the Other Commands menu to use commands that are listed.

> Use the directional keys or Tab⇥ or ⇧Shift + Tab⇥ to move the highlight.

> Your instructor will tell you which collection to expand.

FIGURE 1-17

```
 PINE 3.91   FOLDER LIST                    Folder: INBOX  2 Messages
 ------------------------------------------------------------------------
                       Incoming Message Folders
 ------------------------------------------------------------------------

 INBOX

 ------------------------------------------------------------------------
 Folder-collection <IMAP Server Mail Store>  ** Default for Saves **    (Remote)
 ------------------------------------------------------------------------

 sentmail            saved-messages        sentmail-apr-1995

 ------------------------------------------------------------------------
 Folder-collection <AFS Mail Store>                                     (Local)
 ------------------------------------------------------------------------

                    [ Select Here to See Expanded List ]


 ? Help        M Main Menu  P PrevFldr   - PrevPage   D Delete    R Rename
 O OTHER CMDS  V [ViewFldr] N NextFldr  Spc NextPage  A Add
 ■ general                                                         09:54
```

folder names in collection

The folder named Sentmail should be displayed in the folder list. Open the Sentmail folder.

A message tells you that Pine is closing the Inbox and keeping all messages. The next message tells you that Pine is opening the Sentmail folder.

> To open the folder, move the highlight to the folder name and press ↵Enter.

Once the Sentmail folder is open, your screen should be similar to Figure 1-18.

name of open folder

FIGURE 1-18

header lines for the
messages sent

```
  PINE 3.91    FOLDER INDEX <IMAP Server Mail Store> sentmail  Msg  2 of  2 NEW
 N 1  May 20 To: Colleen.Hayes@    (570) A new message on e-mail
 N 2  May 20 To: COLLEEN.HAYES@    (750) Re: A new message on e-mail
















                    [Folder "sentmail" opened with  2 messages]
 ? Help        M Main Menu  P PrevMsg    - PrevPage   D Delete      R Reply
 O OTHER CMDS  V [ViewMsg]  N NextMsg  Spc NextPage   U Undelete    F Forward
 # general                                                          09:55
```

The same message header line layout as in the Inbox folder appears for each message in the Sentmail folder.

Sometimes you may want to review all the messages you have sent. To do this, you need to open the Out mailbox, which contains copies of all messages you have sent. To close the message window,

Choose: File>Close
   ➤   Ctrl + W

In a similar manner, close the In window.
   To open the Out mailbox,

Choose: Mailbox>Out

Your screen should be similar to Figure 1-19.

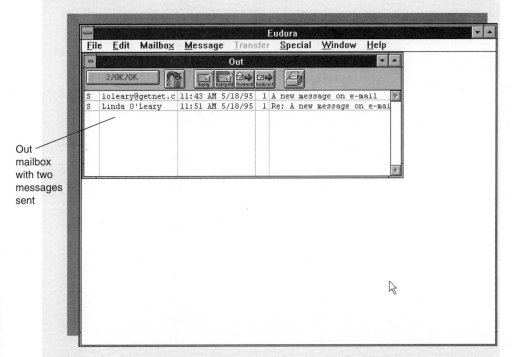

Out
mailbox
with two
messages
sent

FIGURE 1-19

The same message header line layout as in the In mailbox appears for each message in the Out mailbox.

Header lines for the two messages you sent are listed. The Pine status indicator N at the beginning of the message header lines indicates that the messages are new. The Eudora indicator S indicates that the messages were sent. Moving around and viewing the messages is the same as using the Inbox or In mailbox.

Creating an Address Book or Recipient List

Many e-mail programs allow you to create your own file of addresses. In Pine this is called an **address book**, and in Eudora it is called a **recipient list**. This saves time when entering the recipient's address in your e-mail correspondence. (It's like speed-dialing a phone number.) Usually you add addresses to the address book by typing them in directly or by copying the address from the message header of a message you received.

Pine E-Mail

To return to the Main menu,

Type: M (Main Menu)

To see your personal address book,

Type: A (Address Book)

Your screen should be similar to Figure 1-20.

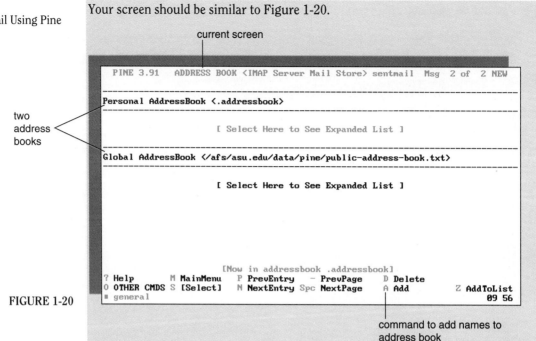

FIGURE 1-20

Depending upon your system setup, your screen may simply display a blank address book, or as shown in Figure 1-20, multiple address books that are already defined. In systems with multiple address books, one is your personal address book and another may be a global address book. A **global address book** is one that is created, updated, and maintained by your system administrator. Generally, this address book contains addresses of e-mail users at that site.

If your system does not have multiple address books, you are automatically placed in the personal address book and can begin adding address entries. In this case, skip to the command "Type: A (Add)" below.

If your Address Book screen is divided into sections, you need to expand the Personal AddressBook section to open your address book. To open your personal address book,

Choose: [Select Here to See Expanded List]

If your address book is empty, "[Empty]" is displayed and highlighted. If your address book contains entries, they are displayed.

To add a new name to your personal address book,

Type: A (Add)

Your screen should be similar to Figure 1-21.

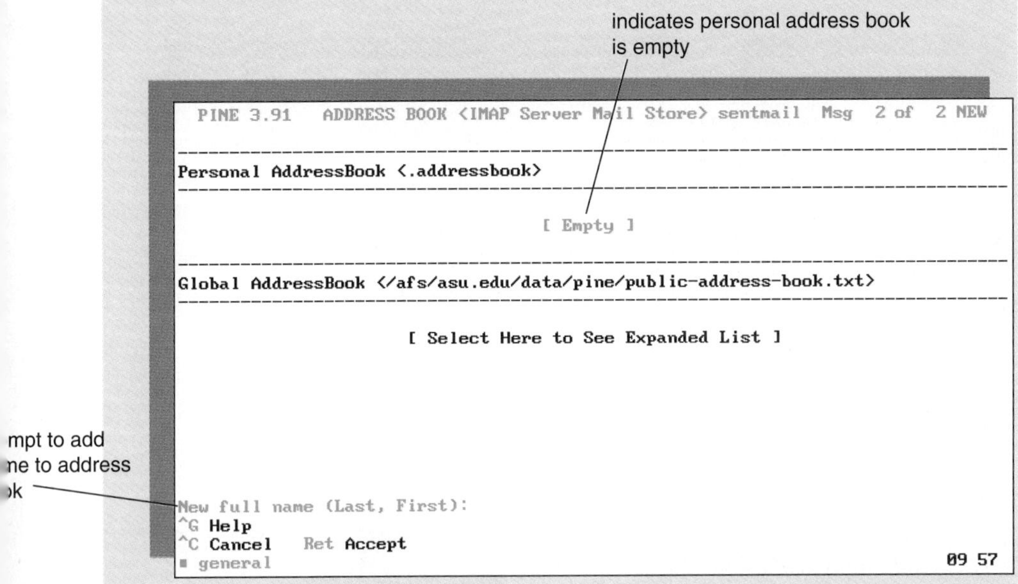

indicates personal address book
is empty

```
    PINE 3.91   ADDRESS BOOK <IMAP Server Mail Store> sentmail  Msg  2 of  2 NEW
───────────────────────────────────────────────────────────────────────────────
Personal AddressBook <.addressbook>
───────────────────────────────────────────────────────────────────────────────
                                  [ Empty ]

───────────────────────────────────────────────────────────────────────────────
Global AddressBook </afs/asu.edu/data/pine/public-address-book.txt>
───────────────────────────────────────────────────────────────────────────────

                      [ Select Here to See Expanded List ]




New full name (Last, First):
^G Help
^C Cancel     Ret Accept
■ general                                                           09 57
```

mpt to add
ne to address
)k

FIGURE 1-21

You will add your instructor's e-mail address to your address book. The prompt "New full name (Last, First)" is displayed. To enter a name,

Type: instructor's last and first names
Press: ⏎ Enter

The next prompt, "Enter new nickname (one word and easy to remember)," is displayed. To help you remember which class this instructor teaches,

Type: course number of the class
Press: ⏎ Enter

In response to the last prompt for the e-mail address,

Type: instructor's e-mail address
Press: ⏎ Enter

Pine tells you that it is writing to the address book. When it is finished, you are notified that the addition is complete and the address book is updated.

Your instructor will provide you with the e-mail address.

If the address you are entering is at your own site, it is not necessary to enter the domain name or code (the part of the address to the right of the @ symbol). Pine will automatically fill this in for you.

Your screen should be similar to Figure 1-22.

instructor's address

```
   PINE 3.91   ADDRESS BOOK <IMAP Server Mail Store> sentmail  Msg  2 of  2 NEW
────────────────────────────────────────────────────────────────────────────────
Personal AddressBook <.addressbook>
────────────────────────────────────────────────────────────────────────────────
CIS200     O'Leary, Timothy                   CIS200@asu.edu
────────────────────────────────────────────────────────────────────────────────
Global AddressBook </afs/asu.edu/data/pine/public-address-book.txt>

                      [ Select Here to See Expanded List ]




                     [Addition complete. Address book updated.]
? Help        M MainMenu    P PrevEntry   - PrevPage     D Delete     S CreateList
O OTHER CMDS  E [Edit]      N NextEntry  Spc NextPage    A Add        Z AddToList
■ general                                                                   09:59
```

FIGURE 1-22

nickname   full name   e-mail address

To add an address to your address book from a message you are viewing, use the T (TakeAddr) command.

You can quickly send a new message from the address book by selecting the address and selecting Compose.

The address you entered is displayed as a line in the address book. Each entry begins with the nickname. The next entry is the full name of the person or organization. The third part is the e-mail address itself. Multiple addresses in your address book are displayed in alphabetical order by last name.

Eudora

To add names and e-mail addresses to the recipient list, you first enter a **nickname**, or short reminder of the recipient, and then enter their e-mail address.

You will add your instructor's name to your recipient list. To do this,

Choose: Window>Nicknames

➤   Ctrl + L

To create a new nickname,

Click: New

The New Nickname dialog box is displayed. To enter a name,

Type: your instructor's name

To add the name to the recipient list,

Select: <u>P</u>ut it on recipient list
Choose: OK

The insertion point is displayed in the Address(es) list box.

Type: instructor's e-mail address

Close the New Nickname dialog box. Save the changes to the nicknames.

> Your instructor will provide you with the e-mail address.

> To close the dialog box, double-click on the control-menu box or press [Ctrl] + [F4].

In the next section you will learn how to use your address book or recipient list.

Forwarding a Message

Another convenient feature of e-mail is the ability to **forward** a message you have received to another person. All that is needed when forwarding a message is to specify the address of the new recipient. The e-mail program automatically includes the text of the message you are forwarding. This saves retyping the same information. You will use the address you entered in your personal address book or recipient list to forward the reply you sent to yourself to your instructor.

Pine E-Mail

To return to the folder list,

Type: L (Folder List)

To close the Sentmail folder and open the Inbox,

Select: INBOX

Then, to view the list of messages,

Type: I (Index)

Select the message header line of the reply message you sent.

Type: F (Forward)

Your screen should be similar to Figure 1-23.

blank recipient line ⎯⎯

indicates a forwarded ⎯
message

forwarded message ⎯⎯
header

forwarded message ⎯⎯
text

FIGURE 1-23

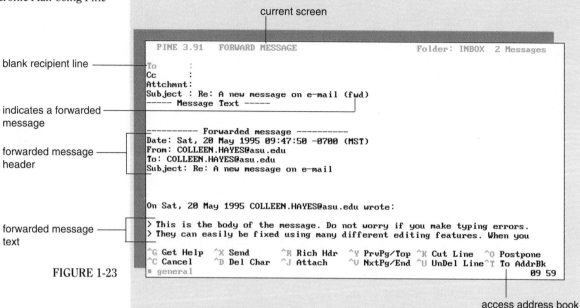

The Forward Message screen displays the message you want to forward in the message text area. It also includes the forwarded message header information. The To line is blank so you can enter the address of the person to whom you want to forward the message. The subject line displays "(fwd)," indicating a forwarded message. To enter your instructor's e-mail address from your personal address book in the To text line,

Press: Ctrl + T (To AddrBk)

If necessary, expand the Personal AddressBook list.

To select an address, highlight the address in the address list. If necessary, highlight your instructor's address.

Press: ←Enter

You can also type the nickname of someone in your address book in the To field. Then when you move off the field, Pine automatically expands the address to the full e-mail address.

You can also search the address books using WhereIs to move to a specific name in the address book.

Your screen should be similar to Figure 1-24.

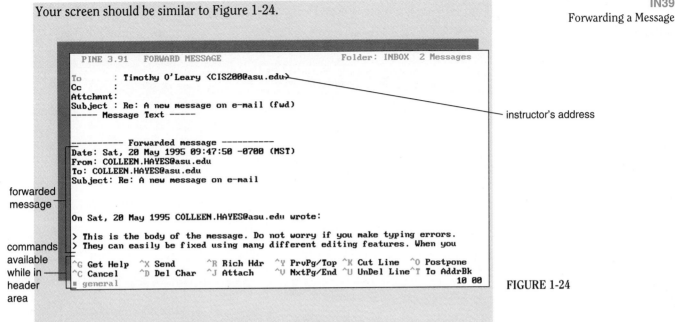

instructor's address

forwarded message

commands available while in header area

FIGURE 1-24

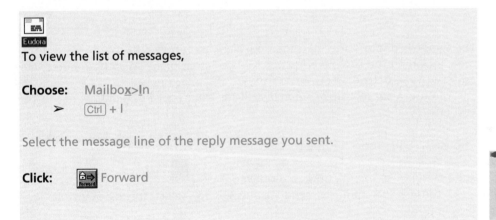

Eudora

To view the list of messages,

Choose: Mailbo**x**>**I**n

➤ Ctrl + I

Select the message line of the reply message you sent.

Click: Forward

The Forward option on the Message menu can also be used to forward a message.

INTERNET

Your screen should be similar to Figure 1-25.

blank recipient line ———

forwarded message ———

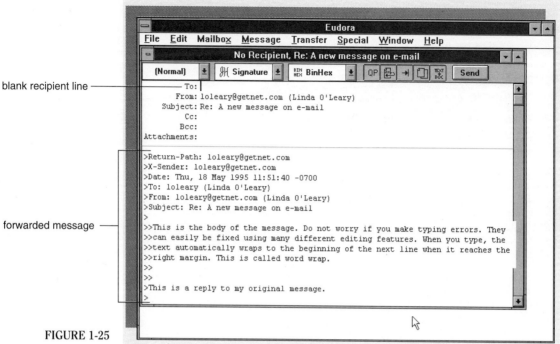

FIGURE 1-25

The window displays the message you want to forward in the message text area, including the complete header. The To line is blank so you can enter the address of the person you want to forward the message to.

To enter your instructor's e-mail address from your Recipient list in the To text line,

Choose: Edit>Insert Recipient

A submenu of recipient names is displayed.

To insert the name to send a message to, select the nickname in the recipient list.

Select your instructor's name.

The name of your instructor appears in the To line. This is much faster than typing the entire address, and also minimizes errors in typing complicated e-mail addresses.

You can add text to the existing message, just as you would if composing a new message or replying to a message. To add a brief message of your own in the body above the forwarded message text, move to a blank line above the forwarded message.

> Pine: The address is also displayed on the To line.

> Eudora: You will need to create a blank line by pressing ⏎Enter at the beginning of the first line.

Type: I am forwarding a copy of the reply I sent to the message.

Send the message.

The message is forwarded to the recipient.

Saving a Message

Some messages you receive will contain information that you will want to keep. To keep a message, you save it as a file. This is also called **archiving**.

Pine E-Mail

You can save a file in Pine e-mail format within the Pine system using the Save command. These files can only be opened using Pine. Alternatively, you can save it as a text file in your home directory or current working directory using the Export command. Then you can open the file using any word processor.

You will save the reply you sent to a file within the Pine e-mail system. If necessary, highlight the message header line of the message you want to save.

The Save and Export commands are menu options under the Other Commands menu.

Type: O (Other Cmds)

To save the message as an e-mail file,

Type: S (Save)

Your screen should be similar to Figure 1-26.

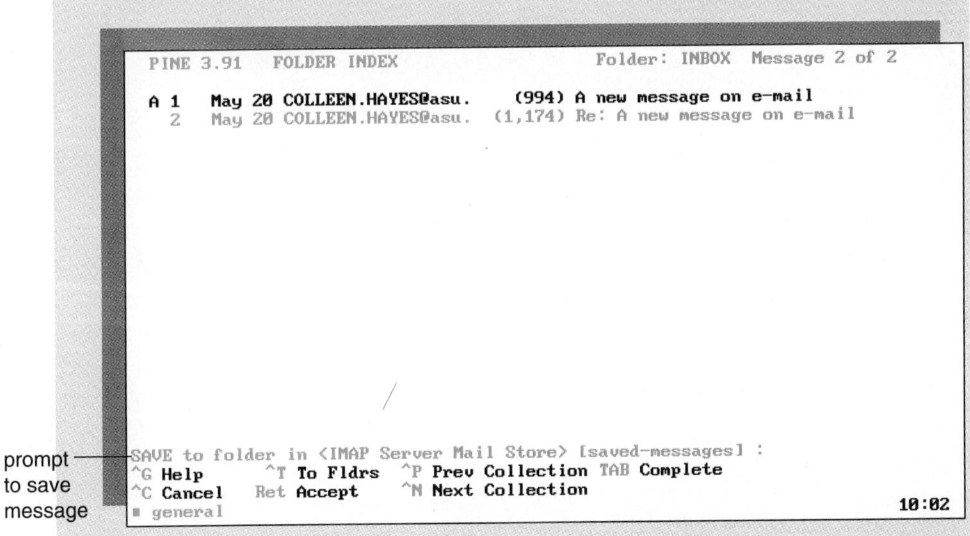

FIGURE 1-26

```
PINE 3.91   FOLDER INDEX                    Folder: INBOX   Message 2 of 2

A 1    May 20  COLLEEN.HAYES@asu.    (994) A new message on e-mail
  2    May 20  COLLEEN.HAYES@asu.  (1,174) Re: A new message on e-mail












SAVE to folder in <IMAP Server Mail Store> [saved-messages] :
^G Help        ^T To Fldrs   ^P Prev Collection TAB Complete
^C Cancel    Ret Accept      ^N Next Collection
# general                                                    10:02
```

prompt to save message

The prompt "SAVE to folder in" is displayed. The name of the default folder for your system appears following the prompt. To save the message in the default folder,

Press: [←Enter]

The message "Message # copied to available folder name in <active mail store> and marked delete" is displayed. When you save a message, the original message is automatically marked for deletion. The D indicator next to the message line indicates the deleted status of this message. The message is saved as a file in e-mail format. You can open the file to view it at any time by opening the Saved-messages folder.

You can also type in the name of another available folder.

INTERNET

Eudora

You would like to save the message to your data disk. Place a disk in the appropriate drive. To save the message to your data disk,

Choose: File>Save As

Your screen should be similar to Figure 1-27.

FIGURE 1-27

default file name ———

Save As dialog box ———

Include Headers ———
option

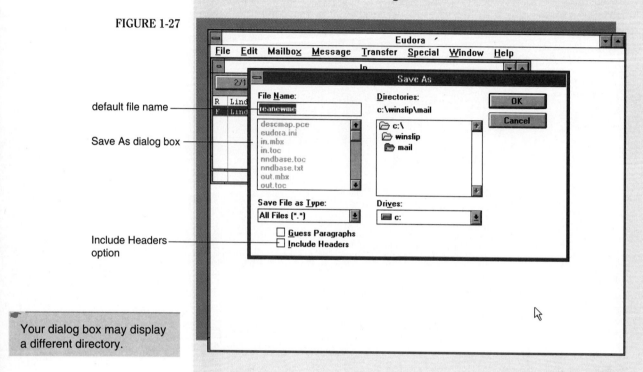

> Your dialog box may display a different directory.

The Save As dialog box is displayed. Notice that the default file name is the first eight characters of the subject line displayed without spaces. You would also like the saved message to contain the header information. To do this,

Select: Include Headers

Next you need to select the drive that contains your data disk. Select the drive that contains your data disk.
    To save the file,

Choose: OK

The file is saved on your data disk. You can open the file using any word processing program.

Deleting a Message

Other messages, once read, are no longer needed. To clear your Inbox of unneeded mail, you can quickly delete messages. Messages are deleted by highlighting the message header line and using the Delete command. You will delete the messages you sent yourself.

Highlight the first message header line.

Pine E-Mail

Press: D (Delete)

A D appears to the left of the header to show that the message status is Deleted. The message is not actually removed, however, until you quit the Pine program. If you want to restore a message that is marked for deletion, highlight the message header and use the ^U Undelete command to remove the D status marker.

Return to the Main menu.

Eudora

Click:

Eudora removes the message from the In mailbox and transfers it to a trash mailbox. It is not permanently deleted until you use the Empty Trash command on the Special menu. You can view messages in the trash mailbox using the Trash command on the Mailbox menu. Then if you want to restore a message that is in the trash mailbox to the In mailbox, you can use the In command on the Transfer menu.

Delete the message you sent to your instructor. Empty the trash mailbox.

> You can also use the Delete command on the Message menu or the shortcuts [Delete] or [Ctrl] + D to delete a message.

Using the Global Address Book (Pine Only)
Pine E-Mail

If your school does not have a global address book, skip this section.

If your school maintains a global address book, you can use it to find addresses of users at your site. To view the global address book,

Type: A (Address Book)

To open the global address book,

Select: [Select Here to See Expanded List] in the Global Address Book section

Your screen should be similar to Figure 1-28.

global address book list

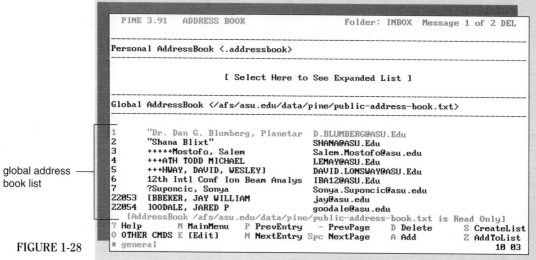

```
   PINE 3.91   ADDRESS BOOK                   Folder: INBOX  Message 1 of 2 DEL
   -----------------------------------------------------------------------------
   Personal AddressBook <.addressbook>
   -----------------------------------------------------------------------------

                       [ Select Here to See Expanded List ]
   -----------------------------------------------------------------------------
   Global AddressBook </afs/asu.edu/data/pine/public-address-book.txt>
   -----------------------------------------------------------------------------
    1       "Dr. Dan G. Blumberg, Planetar  D.BLUMBERG@ASU.Edu
    2       "Shana Blixt"                   SHANA@ASU.Edu
    3       +++++Mostofo, Salem             Salem.Mostofo@asu.edu
    4       +++ATH TODD MICHAEL             LEMAY@ASU.Edu
    5       +++HWAY, DAVID, WESLEY]         DAVID.LONSWAY@ASU.Edu
    6       12th Intl Conf Ion Beam Analys  IBA12@ASU.Edu
    7       ?Suponcic, Sonya                Sonya.Suponcic@asu.edu
   22053    [BBEKER, JAY WILLIAM            jay@asu.edu
   22054    ]OODALE, JARED P                goodale@asu.edu
   __ [AddressBook /afs/asu.edu/data/pine/public-address-book.txt is Read Only]
   ? Help       M MainMenu    P PrevEntry   - PrevPage   D Delete     S CreateList
   O OTHER CMDS E [Edit]      N NextEntry  Spc NextPage  A Add        Z AddToList
   ■ general                                                          10 03
```

FIGURE 1-28

Your screen will display the names and addresses of all the people that have e-mail addresses at your institution. The commands in the command list tell you how to move through the pages of the address book. To see the next page of names,

Press: [Spacebar]

The next set of names is displayed in alphabetical order. If your school is very large, there could be hundreds or even thousands of names in the global address book. It could take you a long time to page through all the names to find someone whose name is at the end of the alphabet. The WhereIs command will help you find a name quickly. To search for a specific name,

Type: O (Other Cmds)
Type: W (WhereIs)

Pine prompts you to enter a word to search for.

> Do not include spaces or apostrophes in names.

Type: a friend or classmate's last name
Press: [←Enter]

> Your instructor may provide you with a name to locate.

After a few seconds, the first occurrence of the name you entered should be displayed. Scroll through the list until you find your friend or classmate. You could now write down the address and add it to your personal address book.
When you are done, return to the Main menu.

> It may take longer to locate a name if the system is busy.

Quitting E-Mail

Pine E-Mail

To end a Pine e-mail session,

Type: Q (Quit)

A prompt to confirm that you really want to quit Pine is displayed.

Type: Y (Yes)

Because you marked two mail messages for deletion, the prompt, "Expunge the 2 deleted messages from the 'Inbox'?" appears. If you respond No, you remain in Pine so you can undelete a message if you wish. If you respond Yes, the messages are removed from the Inbox and you exit the program.

Type: Y (Yes)

Pine closes the open folder and returns you to the system prompt or school menu.

Eudora

Before exiting Eudora, you should close all the open windows. Close any open windows.

To end a Eudora e-mail session,

Choose: File>Exit
  ➢   Ctrl + Q

> You can also quit from the Index screen by typing Q without returning to the Main menu.

Key Terms

e-mail   (IN7)
store-and-forward   (IN7)
address   (IN8)
Domain Name System   (IN8)
attachment   (IN8)
signature line   (IN8)
Netiquette   (IN9)
shout   (IN9)
flame   (IN9)
smiley   (IN10)
emoticon   (IN10)
Pine   (IN10)
folder   (IN11)
status line   (IN11)

Eudora   (IN12)
context-sensitive Help   (IN13)
cursor   (IN14)
header   (IN16)
body   (IN16)
spell checker   (IN19)
status indicator   (IN23)
mailbox   (IN24)
address book   (IN33)
recipient list   (IN33)
global address book   (IN34)
nickname   (IN36)
forward   (IN37)
archive   (IN41)

INTERNET

Command Summary (Pine)

Command	Action
pine	Starts Pine
? or Ctrl + G (Help)	Accesses context-sensitive Help
E (Exit Help)	Exits Help system
C (Compose Message)	Opens Compose Message screen
Ctrl + T (To Spell)	Starts spell checker
Ctrl + X (Send)	Sends a message
L (Folder List)	Displays Folder List screen
J (Jump)	Moves to specified message
V (View Msg)	Displays a message
R (Reply)	Sends a reply to current message
O (Other Cmds)	Displays a menu of additional commands
I (Index)	Displays an index of messages in folder
M (Main Menu)	Returns to Main menu from Help or a folder
A (Address Book)	Opens Address Book screen
A (Add)	Adds a new name to personal address book
F (Forward)	Forwards current message to another recipient
Ctrl + T (To AddrBk)	Adds name from address book to message
S (Save)	Saves a message to specified folder
D (Delete)	Deletes a message from folder
W (WhereIs)	Locates a name in address book
Q (Quit)	Quits Pine

Command Summary (Eudora)

Command	Shortcut	Button	Action
Special>**C**onfiguration			Sets up Eudora with personal information
Message>**N**ew Message	Ctrl + N		Creates a new message
Message>**S**end Immediately	Ctrl + E	Send	Sends a message
File>Check **M**ail	Ctrl + M		Checks for new mail
Message>**R**eply	Ctrl + R	Reply	Sends a reply to current message
File>**C**lose	Ctrl + W		Closes an open window
Mailbo**x**>**O**ut			Opens Out mailbox
Window>**N**icknames	Ctrl + L		Creates a nickname
Mailbo**x**>**I**n	Ctrl + I		Opens In mailbox
Message>**F**orward		Forward	Forwards current message to another recipient
Edit>Insert **R**ecipient			Adds name from recipient list to message
File>Save **A**s			Saves message to a file
Message>**D**elete	Delete or Ctrl + D		Deletes a message
Special>**E**mpty Trash			Permanently deletes message
Transfer>**I**n			Moves message to In mailbox
Mailbox>**T**rash			Displays contents of trash mailbox
File>E**x**it	Ctrl + Q		Quits Eudora

Matching

1. flame _____ a. electronic mail communications over a network

2. archive _____ b. a happy emoticon

3. e-mail _____ c. a text or non-text file that is attached to an e-mail message

4. header _____ d. to send a message on to another recipient

5. doleary@mckenna.com _____ e. rules of courteous e-mail communication

6. forward _____ f. to save a message

7. :=) _____ g. ranting and raving message

8. attachment _____ h. addressing information of an e-mail message

9. Netiquette _____ i. text of an e-mail message

10. body _____ j. an e-mail address

Fill-In Questions

1. Using the sample e-mail message shown below, identify the parts by entering the correct term for each item.

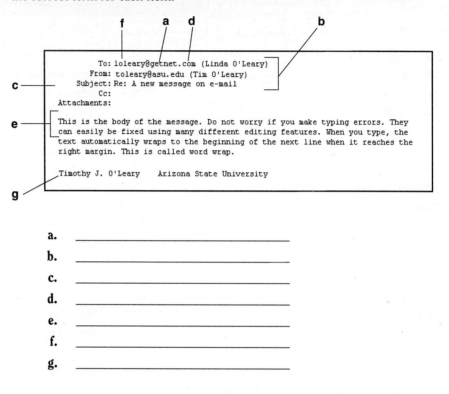

a. _____

b. _____

c. _____

d. _____

e. _____

f. _____

g. _____

Short-Answer Questions

1. What is e-mail? How is e-mail used?

2. What is store-and-forward technology?

3. What is the standard format of an e-mail address?

4. What is an attachment? How do you know if your message includes an attachment? How do you view an attachment?

5. What is a signature line?

6. What are the rules of courteous e-mail correspondence called? Discuss three rules and why they are important.

7. How can you express feelings when corresponding using e-mail? Give three examples.

8. Discuss several sources you can use to find an e-mail address.

9. Discuss the advantages of creating an e-mail address book or recipient list.

10. What are some problems associated with e-mail?

Practice Exercises

1. Damon Lembi works for a computer training company. He has access to the Internet and needs information on when a new product is going to be available. He would like to send an e-mail message to his contact at a software supply company.

    a. Start your e-mail program and compose the following new message:

> To: **\<username@domain name>**
> Subject: **Release of new product**
>
> Body: **Jack,**
>
> **I am interested in finding out when you expect to receive the next upgrade of the word processing program I am currently using. I would like to begin preparing class materials so we are ready to go as soon as the product is available. Any help you may be able to provide is appreciated.**
>
> **Thanks, \<your name>**

Your instructor will supply the address.

INTERNET

b. Check the message for errors and edit as needed. If possible, spell-check the message.

c. Send the message.

2. Joanne Clark uses e-mail to keep in contact with her outside sales representatives. She needs to send a message to two representatives that are attending a conference in another city.

a. Start your e-mail program and compose the following new message:

To: <username@domain name>, <*your* username@domain name>
Subject: **New reporting procedure**

Body: **Hope you are enjoying the conference.**

I need to let you know that the company is implementing a new procedure for reporting sales orders. A new form has been designed to help us keep track of the increase in reorders by specific customers.

The new forms will be delivered to your hotel by FedEx this afternoon. If you have any questions about the new forms, send me a message and I will get back in touch with you.

Have fun and don't get too much sun.

Joanne Clark

> Your instructor will supply the address.

b. Check the message for errors and edit as needed. If possible, spell-check the message.

c. Add a smiley to the message.

d. Send the message.

Wait for the message to be placed in your mailbox. You would now like to reply to Joanne's message and ask her about the new forms.

> Your instructor will supply the first address.

e. Display the message and enter the following reply. (Include the original message with the reply.)

To: <Username@domain name>
Body: **Joanne,**

Do you want the orders that have not been submitted yet transferred to the new forms?

<your name>

f. Send the message.

3. You would like to practice adding names to your address book or recipient list.

    a. Collect e-mail addresses from several friends or classmates.

    b. Add their nicknames and addresses to your address list.

    c. Create and send a message to one of the names in your list.

4. Practice composing and sending messages by sending a message to a classmate. Have a classmate send a message to you. When you receive the message from your classmate, reply to it.

2 Mailing Lists and Newsgroups

INTRODUCTION

In this lab you will learn about two very popular and similar Internet features, mailing lists and newsgroups. Both are discussion groups that allow you to participate in interactive, ongoing discussions with people from all over the world. They provide a great way to exchange ideas and information. It may not all be accurate information, but they are generally a rich resource for learning about a topic.

About Mailing Lists

Mailing lists are e-mail discussion groups. Thousands of mailing lists exist on all imaginable topics. You can participate in these groups only through e-mail. All messages sent to a list are sent to each subscriber's e-mail inbox to read.

Many mailing lists are on the **Bitnet**, an academic network founded in 1981 to link universities by e-mail. The Internet and Bitnet networks are connected by a specialized computer called a **gateway**, which translates e-mail messages sent from one network into the **protocol** (rules that control how software and hardware communicate on a network) used on the other network. Because Bitnet relies heavily on e-mail to move information, you must communicate via e-mail to the mailing lists.

To participate in a mailing list, you first must become a member by subscribing to the list. Most mailing lists are managed by automated computer programs called **listservs**. You subscribe to a mailing list by sending an e-mail message to the **subscription address**, also called the **listserv address**. Listservs may manage more than one mailing list and require that subscribers use a special set of commands to join or leave a list.

Once you have subscribed, your e-mail address is added to the list of subscribers to the mailing list and you will receive copies of all e-mail messages sent to the mailing list. You can then also participate in the discussions by sending e-mail messages to the **list address** of the mailing list. This is different than the subscription address. Try not to confuse the two. Otherwise you may find that you have sent a message to subscribe to all members of the group.

Subscribing to an E-Mail Mailing List

Start the e-mail program and display a blank new message screen.

To subscribe to a list, you must locate the name of the list and the subscription address. One source of mailing list topics is through commercial publications, such as the Internet Yellow Pages published by McGraw-Hill. Several on-line sources are also available that provide mailing list topics. Read the information in the box on on-line mailing list sources.

On-Line Mailing List Sources

To get a list of mailing list topics:

- Send an e-mail message to listserv@bitnic.bitnet. The body of the message should be: "send netinfo filelist or list global." This list may be very long.

- Send an e-mail message to listserv@kentvm.kent.edu (leave the subject line blank). In the body of the message enter "list global."

If you want to limit the list to a specific topic area, in the message body enter "list global/<topic>" (replace "topic" with a word or words describing the subject). For example, to get a list of mailing lists on space, you would enter "list global/space."

Having used one of the mailing list sources, you have decided to subscribe to a discussion group on music. The subscription address of a mailing list consists of listserv@ followed by the listserv address. Those groups that are on the Bitnet use a Bitnet address. Bitnet addresses are different from Internet addresses in that they do not end in geographical or administrative domain names, such as .edu. Generally, all that is needed to send an e-mail message from the Internet to the Bitnet is to add .bitnet to the end of the address. Otherwise you may need to provide the name of the gateway computer and information about how to deliver the mail on Bitnet. Some Bitnet listservs are also connected to the Internet, so if you see a listserv address ending in .edu, you can e-mail the listserv without adding .bitnet to the end. The subscription address for the music mailing list is listserv@american.edu. To subscribe, in the To line,

Type: listserv@american.edu

Most listservs require that you leave the Subject line blank in a message to a listserv.

In your e-mail subscription message, you enter the command to subscribe. When corresponding with the listserv, because you are communicating with a computer program, only certain commands are acknowledged. Because listserv programs vary, different commands may be used by different listservs. The box on the next page describes many of the commands that can be used when sending an e-mail message to most listservs.

Listserv Command	Action
subscribe <listname> <your name>	Subscribes to list
unsubscribe <listname>	Unsubscribes to list
signoff<listname>	Unsubscribes to list
review <listname>	Requests a membership list
index <listname>	Requests names of files that are archived on the list
info <listname>	Requests information about the listserv
get <filename>	Requests a copy of an archived file
set <listname> nomail *or* postpone	Temporarily stops mail delivery
set <listname> mail *or* mail ack	Begins mail delivery again after stopping
set <listname>repro	Has listserv send a copy of whatever you post to list

The subscription message is entered in the message text area. The most common command to begin a subscription is "subscribe." The command is followed by the name of the mailing list. The mailing list name is the part of the mailing address before the @ sign in the list address. The mailing list address for the music mailing list is allmusic@listserv.american.edu. The name of the music mailing list is ALLMUSIC. The mailing list name is then followed by your name. Do not use your e-mail address, because the listserv gets it from your message header.

In the message text area,

Type: subscribe allmusic <your name>

Your screen should be similar to Figure 2-1.

The figures in the mailing list section of this lab reflect the use of the Pine e-mail program. Your screens will show the e-mail program you are using.

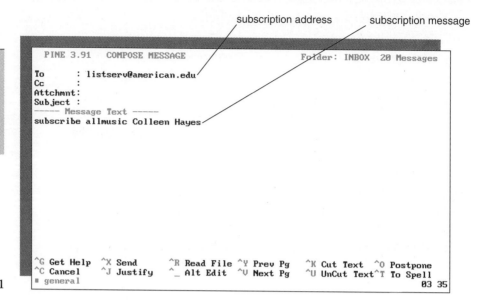

FIGURE 2-1

The subscription message is complete.

Send the message.

Generally, in a matter of a few minutes, you will receive messages back from the listserv. You could receive any number of different responses. One message may tell what computer resources were used to process your subscription. There may be an interim message telling you that your subscription request has been received and that it will be processed shortly or that it is being forwarded. If your subscription request contained an error, you will receive a message indicating what is wrong. In that case, you would need to resubmit your request. Some mailing lists send a message asking you to send a confirmation response to the listserv. If you receive this type of message, you would need to follow the instructions to confirm your subscription.

While waiting for your reply, open your inbox and display your incoming mail messages. Select two mailing lists that are of interest to you from the lists in the boxes on pages IN55 and IN75. In the spaces below, write the subscription address and the subscription message to subscribe to the newsgroups you have selected.

Depending upon the list you subscribe to, it may take minutes or days to receive a reply to your subscription message. You should check your inbox within 48 hours so that a confirmation message does not expire.

Subscription Address   **Subscription Message**

_____   _____

_____   _____

If your subscription request to the music mailing list went through without any problems, you will receive two replies rather quickly.

Note: If you do not receive a reply in ten minutes, continue reading the information in this section. Then continue the lab beginning with the next section on newsgroups. Before ending the lab, check your inbox for replies to your subscription request and perform the instructions in this section.

When your e-mail program indicates that you have received a new message(s), read the first message.

Your screen should be similar to Figure 2-2.

If you receive a reply that this mailing list is not found, try sending a subscription to one of the alternate mailing lists you selected on page 52.

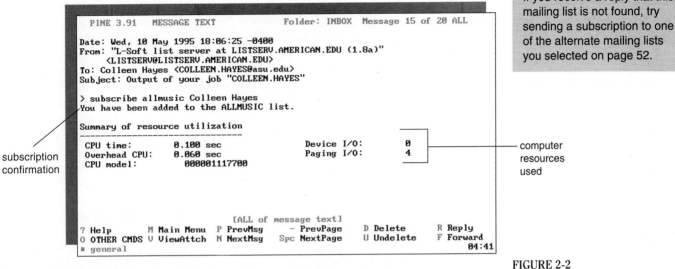

FIGURE 2-2

This first message indicates that you have been added to the ALLMUSIC list.

After a slightly longer time, a second message should be received. Read the second message. Your screen should be similar to Figure 2-3.

```
     PINE 3.91   MESSAGE TEXT            Folder: INBOX   Message 16 of 20 28%

    Date: Wed, 10 May 1995 18:06:24 -0400
    From: "L-Soft list server at LISTSERV.AMERICAN.EDU (1.8a)"
          <LISTSERV@LISTSERV.AMERICAN.EDU>
    Reply to: ALLMUSIC-Request@LISTSERV.AMERICAN.EDU
    To: Colleen Hayes <COLLEEN.HAYES@asu.edu>
    Subject: You are now subscribed to the ALLMUSIC list

    Wed, 10 May 1995 18:06:24

    Your subscription to the ALLMUSIC list  (Discussions on all forms of Music) has
    been accepted.

    Please  save  this  message  for future  reference, especially  if  you are  not
    familiar with LISTSERV. This might look like  a waste of disk space now, but in
    6 months you will be glad you  saved this information when you realize that you
    cannot  remember  what  are  the  lists you  are subscribed  to, or  what is  the
    command to  leave the list to  avoid filling up  your mailbox while you  are on
    vacations.  In fact,  you  should create  a new  mail folder for  subscription
    confirmation messages  like this one, and  for the "welcome messages"  from the

    ? Help          M Main Menu  P PrevMsg     - PrevPage    D Delete      R Reply
    O OTHER CMDS  V ViewAttch  N NextMsg   Spc NextPage    U Undelete    F Forward
    ▪ general                                                            04:49
```

FIGURE 2-3

This message welcomes you to the list and provides additional information about the list, including information on how to unsubscribe. You will want to save a copy of this message so you will know how to unsubscribe to the list at a later time.

Refer to Lab 1 if you need
help on saving the message.

When you receive your welcome message indicating that you are subscribed to the list, save the message.

Delete all other replies you received from the listserv.

Now you will begin receiving copies of all new e-mail messages sent to this mailing list. Depending on how active the list is, you may begin receiving messages immediately and you may find that your inbox is flooded with e-mail messages from the mailing list. When you first subscribe, you may want to observe and find out what the list is about before participating. Each list has its own personality. If you do not like it, you can unsubscribe.

When sending or **posting** a message such as a question to the mailing list, the e-mail message is sent to the list address, not the subscription address. The list address consists of the list name followed by @ and the last part of the subscription address. In this case, you would address your e-mail message to allmusic@american.edu.

Any e-mail messages you send to the list will be sent to all list members unless you address the message to an individual. Be careful when sending your reply that the reply is sent to the appropriate location.

It is possible that a topic you are interested in may have already been discussed, and someone may refer you to a past posting on the list. Many of these past postings are saved (archived) by the listserv. Requesting an information sheet from the listserv will usually provide instructions on how to access archived postings (see command list on page IN51).

When corresponding in a mailing list, keep the following rules of etiquette in mind:

- Keep your questions and comments relevant to the focus of the list.

- Remember, what you say is seen by all members of the list. If your reply would have meaning only to the sender of an e-mail message, send your reply to the individual rather than to the list.

- Keep the number of lists you subscribe to small. The messages from various listservs require extensive system processing and can tie up computer resources. In addition, your mailbox may suddenly become very full.

- When asking a question, you can request that responses be sent to you personally rather than to the list. Then you can compile a summary of the answers to share with the entire list if you want.

- When replying, check that your response is going to the correct location, that is, to the list or the individual.

- When you go on vacation, unsubscribe or suspend mail delivery.

To unsubscribe to the
music mailing list, send the
message "signoff allmusic" to
listserv@listserv.american.edu.

After waiting a few days and reading some of the messages you receive from the mailing list, if you find you are interested in a topic, post a message to the mailing list (use the list address). If you are not interested, send a message back to the subscription address unsubscribing to the list.

A sampling of mailing list topics with their addresses is shown in the box below.

Topic	Subscription Address (listserv@)	List Name
Aquariums (hobby)	emuvm1.cc.emory.edu	AQUARIUM
Art reviews (books, music)	columbia.ilc.com	BOOKNEWS
Computer-aided design (manufacturing)	suvm.syr.edu	CADAM-L
Highlander (TV-movie)	psuvm.psu.edu	HIGHLA-L
Cruise the net (Internet)	unlvm.bitnet	CRUISE-L
Music	gitvm1.bitnet	RMUSIC-L
Wild birds	arizvm1.ccit.arizona.edu	BIRDBAND
Biosphere	ubvm.cc buffalo.edu	BIOSPH-L
Japanese food/culture	jpnku01.bitnet	J-FOOD
Vegetarianism	gibbs.oit.unc.edu	VEGGIE
Exercise & sports psychology	vm.temple.edu	SPORTPSY
Star Trek	pccvm.bitnet	STREK-L

Because mailing lists come and go, some of these lists may no longer be available. Check the end of the lab for additional listserv names.

When you have completed this section, exit your e-mail program.

About Newsgroups

Newsgroups are discussion groups that are similar to mailing lists, but the e-mail messages are not sent to your personal inbox. Instead they are posted to newsgroup sites. A **newsgroup site** is a computer that participates in the network news system. Each site receives one copy of messages, called **articles**, that are posted each day. The articles are stored on the site's disk, and after a period of time are removed. The length of time articles are displayed is controlled by the news administrator at the site. The news administrator also decides what discussion groups to carry.

The connection between newsgroup sites creates a network called **Usenet**. It is estimated that about 10 million computer newsgroup sites are on-line. There are more than 1500 newsgroups, with new ones being added all the time (and others being removed).

There are two types of newsgroups, moderated and unmoderated. In **moderated newsgroups**, articles are sent to the moderator, who reviews or screens them for appropriateness before they are distributed. In **unmoderated newsgroups**, the articles are not screened. Anyone can start a newsgroup on any topic. Generally, they consist of open and uncensored discussions.

A **newsreader** program is needed to subscribe to and participate in newsgroups. The newsreader program helps you keep track of the articles you have read and displays new articles that have arrived since you were last in the newsgroup. On Unix systems, the most common newsreader program is *rn*. **Trumpet** is a newsreader program with a Windows interface.

You subscribe to newsgroups in order to participate in the discussion. Subscribing to a newsgroup adds the newsgroup to your personal list of newsgroups, which is displayed when you start the newsreader program. You can read articles in a newsgroup at any time even if you are not subscribed.

Usenet organizes newsgroups into categories called **hierarchies**. There are about a dozen major top-level hierarchies. See the box below for a description of the top-level hierarchies.

Hierarchy	Description
alt	Alternative topics — miscellaneous discussions that generally inspire a lot of different opinions
bionet	Biology
comp	Computers
biz	Business
K12	Education
rec	Recreation
soc	Social issues
sci	Science
talk	Controversial topics
misc	Discussions that do not fit anywhere else
news	Discussions about netnews itself

Newsgroups have multi-part names separated by dots. The names reflect the order of focus with the main topic first, separated from the next (subtopic) by a dot, and so forth. The most general name (top level of hierarchy) is on the left and the most specific is on the right. Therefore, as you read from left to right, the various parts of the name progressively narrow the topic of discussion. For example, the newsgroup comp.unix.questions deals with questions on using Unix, and the newsgroup alt.fan.monty-python is a discussion group devoted to the British comedy troupe.

Many newsgroups also include a frequently-asked-questions (**FAQ**) article. This article contains answers to the most frequently asked questions on the topic and also explains abbreviations that you will see are frequently used in the newsgroup (such as SO for significant other).

A sample of some newsgroups and their discussion areas is shown in the box below.

Topic	Newsgroup Name	Discussion Area
alt	alt.romance	Romance-related discussions, such as how to ask someone out
	alt.tv.northern-exp	Northern Exposure television program
	alt.sexy.bald.captains	Patrick Stewart fans
rec	rec.food.recipes	Recipe exchange
	rec.travel	Basic advice and tips
	rec.travel.france	Travel information on France
	rec.travel.air	Deals on air tickets and other bargains
	rec.travel.marketplace	Deals on air tickets and other bargains
	rec.rollercoaster	Fans of roller coasters exchange experiences
comp	comp.unix.questions	Questions on Unix
	comp.os.msdos	Discussions on OS/MS DOS
	comp.edu	Computer science education
soc	soc.politics	Political problems, systems, solutions
	soc.feminism	Feminism and feminist issues
	soc.college	College activities
news	news.announce.important	Important messages to all Usenet users
	news.answers	FAQs on Usenet
	news.announce.newusers	Standard set of articles with general information about Usenet

INTERNET

Finding and Subscribing to Newsgroups Using Trumpet

If necessary, load Windows.

Generally, the Trumpet newsreader program is found in a program group with other Internet tools. This group may have a name such as Net Tools or Internet Winsock Applications.

Open the program group that contains Trumpet.

To start Trumpet,

> This text assumes schools have a Windows version of the Trumpet newsreader program.

Double-click:
Trumpet

The first time you use Trumpet, the Trumpet Setup dialog box is displayed.

Your screen should be similar to Figure 2-4.

FIGURE 2-4

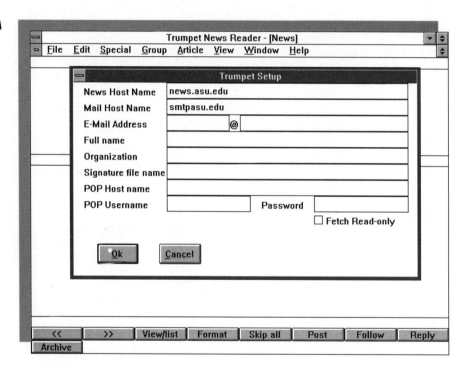

The dialog box displays the News Host Name and the Mail Host Name for your school. The News Host Name is where your school accesses the news files, and the Mail Host Name is where the mail is sent and received.

> The News Host Name and Mail Host Name will reflect the news and mail sites at your school.

To set up Trumpet to maintain information on the newsgroups you subscribe to, you need to enter your e-mail address and name in the dialog box. In the E-Mail Address text box to the left of the @,

Type:　your user name

To complete the e-mail address the right of the @,

Press : [Tab ⇥]

Type: your domain name

To move to and enter your name in the Full Name text box,

Press: [Tab ⇥]

Type: your full name

Complete the Organization text box by entering the name of your school.
    Your screen should be similar to Figure 2-5.

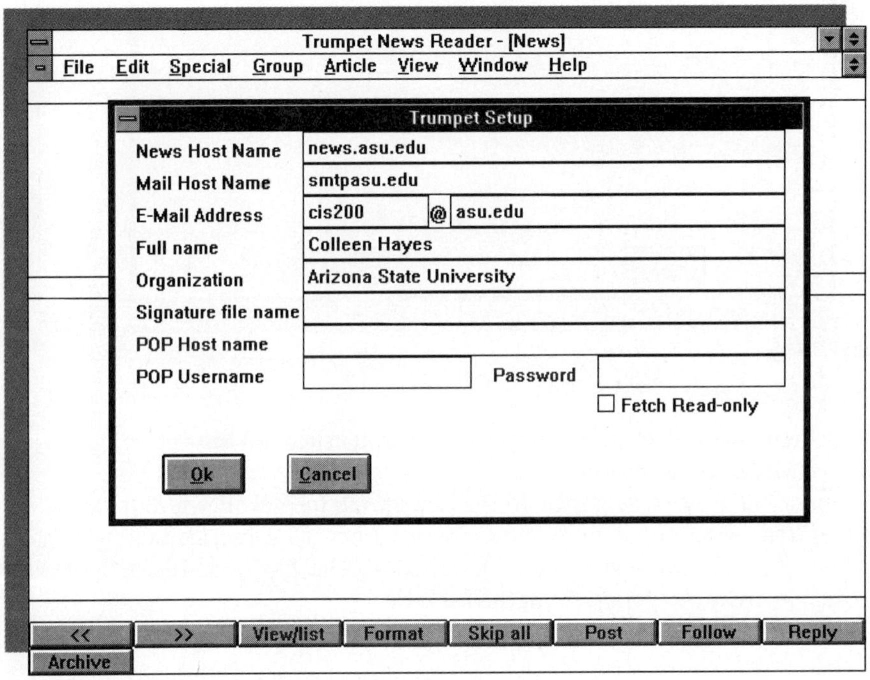

FIGURE 2-5

If you need to complete the information in the other text boxes, your instructor will
provide directions.
    To close the dialog box,

Choose: OK

Your screen should be similar to Figure 2-6.

FIGURE 2-6

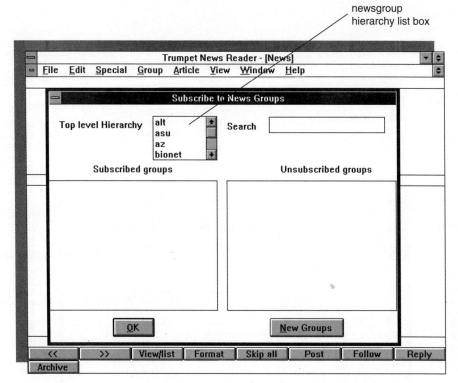

Trumpet automatically connects to your newsgroup site, and the Subscribe to News Groups dialog box is displayed.

First you want to subscribe to the newsgroup for new newsgroup users. The name of this newsgroup is news.announce.newusers. To subscribe to a newsgroup, first you select the category you are interested in. The Top Level Hierarchy list box lists the hierarchy categories. From the list box,

> If the Subscribe to News Groups dialog box is not displayed, select Subscribe from the Group menu.

> If necessary, scroll the list box until "news" is displayed.

Select: news

Note: Your setup may have automatically subscribed you to all newsgroups. In this case, the Subscribe dialog box will not appear and your screen will be similar to Figure 2-10. If this is the case, select "Zap all subscribed groups" from the Special menu, then select Subscribe from the Group menu to subscribe to selected newsgroups.

Your screen should be similar to Figure 2-7.

selected
hierarchy

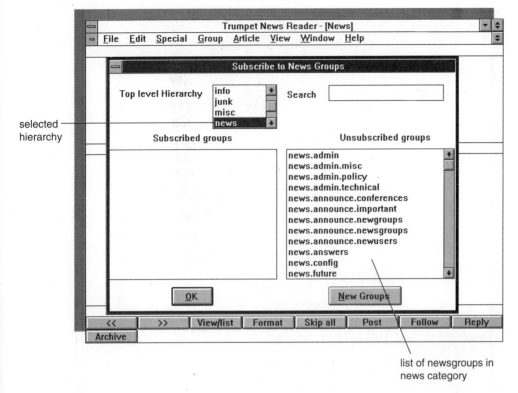

FIGURE 2-7

list of newsgroups in
news category

The Unsubscribed Groups list box now displays a list of newsgroups in the news
category. You want to subscribe to the group that provides information for new
users. To select a newsgroup to subscribe to, click the newsgroup name.

Select: news.announce.newusers

If necessary, scroll the list of
names to locate the news-
group name.

INTERNET

Your screen should be similar to Figure 2-8.

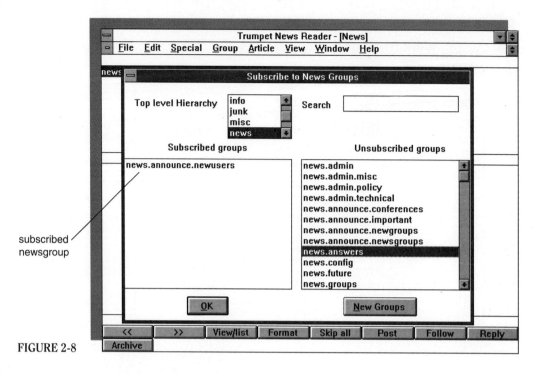

subscribed newsgroup

FIGURE 2-8

The name of the selected newsgroup moved from the Unsubscribed Groups list box to the Subscribed Groups list box.

You have heard about a group that contains thousands of reviews of all popular movies from a variety of critics. You would like to subscribe to this group. Most likely, this group is in the recreation category. From the Top Level Hierarchy list box,

Select: rec

Now the Unsubscribed Groups list box displays newsgroups in the recreation category. The recreation category is divided into many other subcategories. Movie reviews are frequently found in the arts subcategory. Instead of scrolling the list of newsgroup names, you can use the Search text box to move to a newsgroup. In the Search text box,

Type: arts.mo

Your screen should be similar to Figure 2-9.

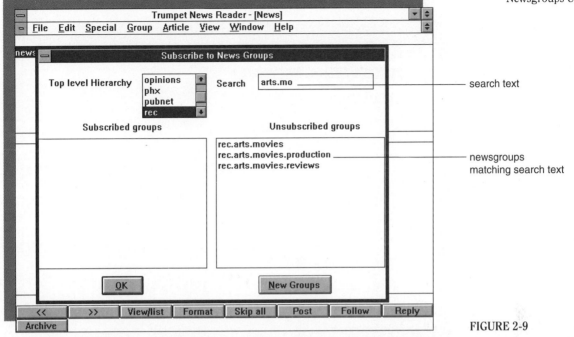

FIGURE 2-9

The Unsubscribed Groups list displays only the newsgroups whose names begin with arts.mo. As you type each character, the unsubscribed list removes any name that does not match the text you have typed. From the newsgroup list,

Select: rec.arts.movies.reviews

This newsgroup name is now displayed in the Subscribed Groups list box.

Next, subscribe to the newsgroup alt.comedy.standup.

If you are interested in subscribing to any other newsgroups, you can subscribe to them now. When you are done subscribing to newsgroups,

Choose: OK

> Your instructor may ask you to subscribe to other newsgroups.

> To subscribe to more newsgroups at a later time, use the Subscribe command on the Group menu.

INTERNET

Your screen should be similar to Figure 2-10.

menu bar

subscribed
newsgroups

button bar

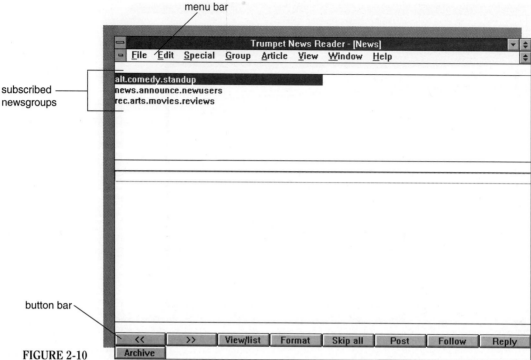

FIGURE 2-10

This may be slow if you
selected a large number of
newsgroups.

Trumpet's main window appears and displays the list of newsgroups you subscribed to in the upper section of the window. The menu bar contains commands that can be used to create and view messages. The button bar at the bottom of the screen is used to navigate through articles and newsgroups and provides shortcuts for many of the frequently used menu commands.

Reading Articles

The main reason for subscribing to newsgroups is to read the articles from other group members. To view the articles in a newsgroup, you select the newsgroup by double-clicking the newsgroup name in the list.

Select: news.announce.newusers

After Trumpet has completed scanning for articles, your screen should be similar to Figure 2-11.

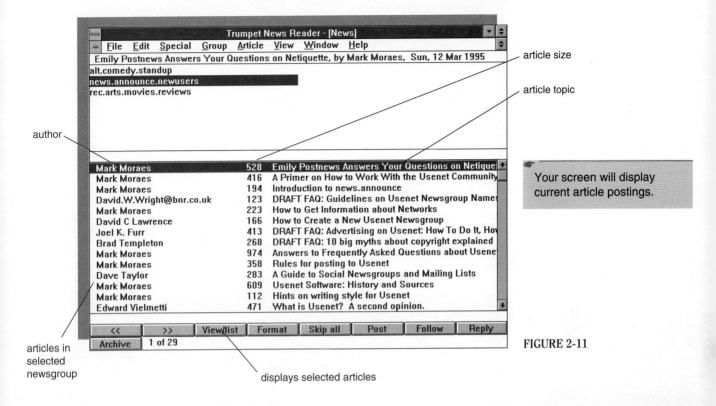

FIGURE 2-11

A list of articles appears in the bottom section of the window. The name of the person who submitted the article appears in the first column. The size of the article in bytes appears in the center column. The topic is the information from the subject line of the article. The article "Introduction to news.announce" includes information for all new users of newsgroups. It is reposted every month with new or updated information.

To read a specific article, highlight the article and click the [**View/list**] button. View the Introduction to news.announce article. If this article is not available, view an article of your choice.

You can also double-click on the article to view it.

A FAQ article is also a good source of information about a topic.

Your screen should be similar to Figure 2-12.

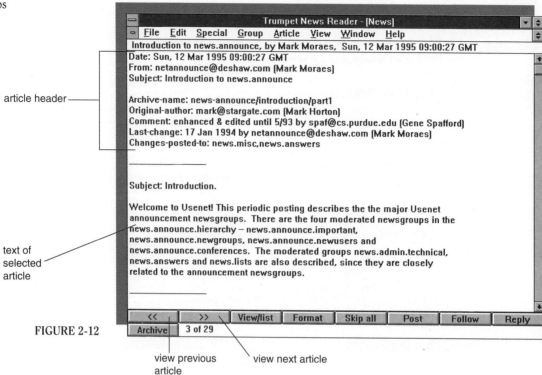

article header —

text of
selected
article

FIGURE 2-12

view previous   view next article
article

Use the scroll bar or ↓ or ↑ to move more text onto the screen.

The button is used to view the previous article.

Clicking toggles between the list window and the view window.

The contents of the selected article appear in a full-screen view window. Read the article.

To view the next article,

Click: `>>`

When you are done reading articles, to return to the list window,

Choose: `View/list`

To look at the articles posted in the movies.reviews newsgroup,

Select: rec.arts.movies.reviews

The list now displays postings to this group. Select and read a few articles in this category. Return to the list window.

Next you would like to view the articles in the comedy.standup newsgroup. Select the alt.comedy.standup newsgroup.

Your screen should be similar to Figure 2-13.

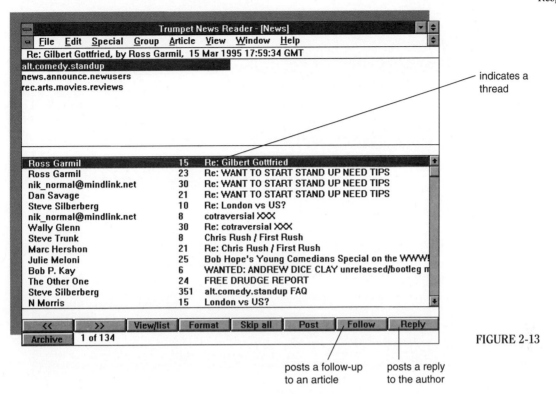

indicates a thread

FIGURE 2-13

posts a follow-up to an article

posts a reply to the author

Notice that this newsgroup contains several article titles that begin with "Re:." This indicates that the article is a response to an original article, thereby creating a discussion thread. **Threads** are newsgroup discussions about a specific topic with a common theme. Threads help organize subtopics in a newsgroup and are used to keep all the articles on the same subject together. When an original article is posted, it begins a new thread. All responses or follow-up articles are attached to the original so that you can read all the articles on the same subject one after the other.

Read an original article and follow the thread through the replies.

Responding to Articles

As you read articles in a newsgroup, you may come across a question for which you have an answer or a topic on which you have an opinion you would like to contribute. To do this you can reply to the article. This is very similar to replying to an e-mail message. With any article displayed,

Choose: Follow

The Reply button is used to send a reply to the author of the article only.

INTERNET

Your screen should be similar to Figure 2-14.

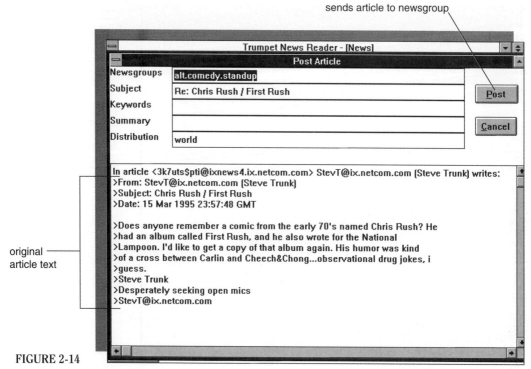

FIGURE 2-14

The Post Article window is displayed. The original article text appears preceded with
>. This distinguishes the original text from the new text you will enter. Your reply
should be entered below the old text. When posting replies, keep them brief and to
the point, being particularly careful to stick to the topic thread. Use the same rules
of etiquette that apply to mailing lists. Once a reply is entered, the Post button is
used to send it. However, in this case you will not send a reply and will cancel this
procedure.

Choose: Cancel

In response to the prompt,

Choose: Y (Yes)

To return to the main listing of articles,

Choose: View/list

Your screen should be similar to Figure 2-15.

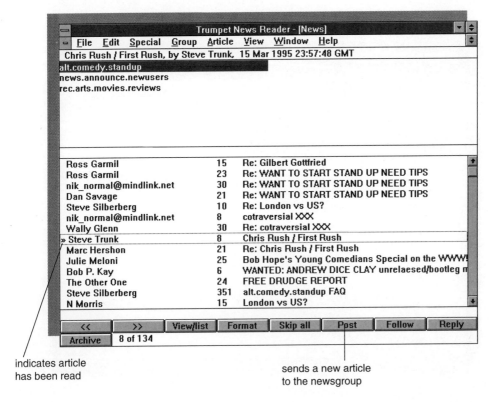

FIGURE 2-15

indicates article
has been read

sends a new article
to the newsgroup

Notice that the articles you have read are preceded with >>. This symbol indicates that the article has been read and will not be displayed the next time you open this newsgroup.

In addition to replying to articles, you may want to start a new article on a new topic thread. To do this, first select the newsgroup you want to send an article to. The comedy newsgroup should already be selected. To compose and post a new article to this newsgroup,

Choose: Post

> To unmark read messages, use the Unread command on the Group menu.

Your screen should be similar to Figure 2-16.

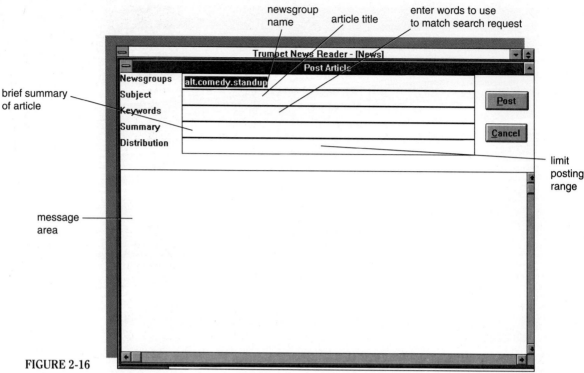

FIGURE 2-16

The Post Article window is displayed. The Newsgroups text box displays the name of the selected newsgroup. In the Subject line you should enter a short descriptive title for your article. The contents of the Subject line help organize articles into threads. The Keyword line is used to enter words that would be used to match a search request. The Summary line is used to enter a short summary of the article. The Distribution line is used to limit the posting range. Leaving the Distribution line blank sends the posting to all members of the newsgroup. You can limit the posting range by typing World, North America, US, State, City, or Local.

In the message area you would enter the text of your message. Just as when you reply to an article, to send a posting, click Post. In this case, however, you will again cancel the procedure.

Choose: Cancel
Choose: Y (Yes)

The list window is displayed again.

After watching the information flow in various newsgroups for a while, you will feel comfortable posting your messages and questions. This may lead to gathering names and exchanging information with many people in different areas of the world. You can also print, copy, cut, and paste messages using the commands in the menu, just as in other Windows applications.

To end your Trumpet session,

Choose: F (File)
Choose: X (Exit)

Key Terms

mailing list   (IN53)
Bitnet   (IN53)
gateway   (IN53)
protocol   (IN53)
listserv   (IN53)
subscription address   (IN53)
listserv address   (IN53)
list address   (IN53)
post   (IN58)
newsgroup   (IN59)

newsgroup site   (IN59)
article   (IN59)
Usenet   (IN59)
moderated newsgroup   (IN59)
unmoderated newsgroup   (IN59)
newsreader   (IN60)
Trumpet   (IN60)
hierarchy   (IN60)
FAQ   (IN60)
thread   (IN71)

Command Summary

Command	Action
Group>**S**ubscribe	Opens Subscribe to News Groups dialog box
Follow	Posts a reply to newsgroup
Reply	Posts a reply to author of article
View/List	Toggles between display of an article or list of articles
Post	Sends a reply
File>**Ex**it	Closes Trumpet program

Matching

1. subscription address _____ a. used to separate topics in a newsgroup name
2. unsubscribe _____ b. e-mail discussion groups
3. Bitnet _____ c. indicates a follow-up article
4. mailing lists _____ d. common theme discussions
5. . (dot) _____ e. address used to subscribe to a mailing list
6. list address _____ f. a collection of thousands of discussion groups
7. post _____ g. to remove your address from a mailing list
8. threads _____ h. address used to send messages to a mailing list
9. Usenet _____ i. network that links universities
10. Re: _____ j. to send a message to a mailing list

Fill-In Questions

1. Using the screen below, enter the correct term for each item.

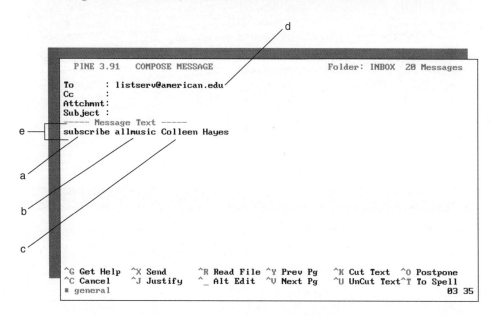

a. _____

b. _____

c. _____

d. _____

e. _____

2. Using the screen below, enter the correct term for each item.

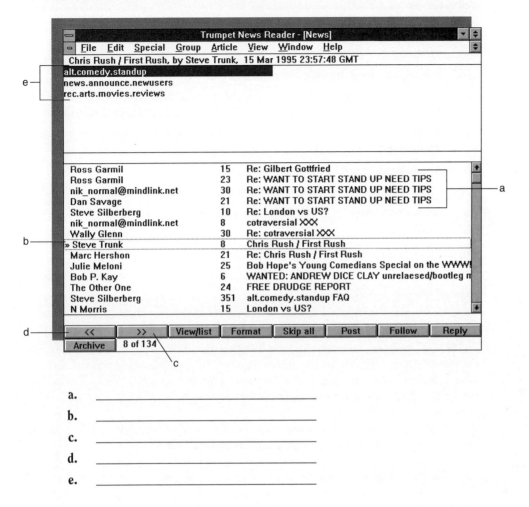

a. _____

b. _____

c. _____

d. _____

e. _____

Short-Answer Questions

1. What is a mailing list?

2. What is a newsgroup?

3. How is a mailing list different from a newsgroup?

4. You want to subscribe to a mailing list on wild birds with a list address of birdband@arizvm1.ccit.arizona.edu. How do you subscribe to this list?

5. What types of responses might you receive from a subscription request to a mailing list?

6. What does it mean to subscribe to a newsgroup?

7. What is the difference between a moderated and unmoderated newsgroup?

8. What do the parts of newsgroup names separated by dots signify?

9. What different ways can you use to respond to a newsgroup article?

10. How do you send a new article to a newsgroup?

Practice Exercises

1. Subscribe to the misc.test newsgroup. Read some of the articles and then create your own test message. Include in either the subject line or in the message the word "ignore." This stops the automatic reply to your message from the servers. Wait a few minutes and see if your message has been posted. (You will need to rescan the article list to see if yours is displayed.)

2. Find the names of two newsgroups on the topic of computers. Describe the types of articles sent to these groups. Do these groups contain threads?

3. Find a newsgroup about the state or country you live in. What is the name of this newsgroup? What types of topics are discussed in this group? Select a topic and describe the types of postings that it contains.

4. Using the list of newsgroups in the box on page IN76 or others of your choice, select a newsgroup, and read and post messages to it.

5. Using the list of mailing lists shown in the box on page IN75, join a group. Check for messages frequently and remember to unsubscribe or postpone your mail when you are not able to check messages.

Additional Mailing List Groups

Category	Topic	Subscription Address (listserv@)	List Name
Art	Ceramics	ukcc.uky.edu	clayart
	Fine art	rutvm1.rutgers.edu	fine-art
Aviation	Aircraft	grearn.csi.forth.gr	aircraft
	Ultralight flying	ms.uky.edu	ultralight-flight
Books	Rare books	rutvm1.rutgers.edu	exlibris
Business	China import/export	ifcss.org	china-link
	Japanese business	pucc.princeton.edu	japan
Comic books	X-men	netcom.com	stripe-l
Computers	Future culture	uafsysb.uark.edu	futurec
	Tipsheet	wsuvm1.csc.wsu.edu	tipsheet
Dance	Folk and traditional	nic.surfnet.nl	dance-l
Economics	Economics	hasarall.bitnet	corryfee
	Marketing	nervm.nerdc.ufl.edu	market-1
Education	Adult literacy	nysernet.org	learner
	Computer networking	tamvm1.tamu.edu	cneduc-l
Gardening	Bonsai	waynest1.bitnet	bonsai
	Home gardening	ukcc.uky.edu	gardens
Health	Drug and alcohol	lmuacad.bitnet	alcohol
Humor	Contemporary	uga.cc.uga.edu	humor
	Giggles	vtvm1.cc.vt.edu	giggles
Jobs	Federal jobs	dartcms1.dartmouth.edu	fedjobs
Medicine	Cystic fibrosis	yalevm.cis.yale.edu	cystic-l
	Nursing	kentvm.kent.edu	gradnrse
Science	Fraud	uacsc2.albany.edu	scifraud
Television	Doctor Who	uel.ac.uk	drwho-l
	Dr.Quinn, Medicine Woman	emuvm1.cc.emory.edu	dqmw
Women	Feminism	mach1.wlu.ca	femisa
	Menopause	psuhms.maricopa.edu	menopaus
World cultures	Central European	aearn.edvz.univie.ac.at	cerro-l
	Friends and partners	solar.rtd.utk.edu	friends
	Native American	tamvm1.tamu.edu	native-l

INTERNET

Additional Newsgroups

Category	Newsgroup Name	Discussion Area
Business	misc.invest	Investments
College	alt.college.us	Rumors and reputations of various schools
Comics	rec.arts.comics.xbooks alt.comics.batman alt.comics.superman	X-men comics Batman comics Superman comics
Dance	rec.art.dance	General dance
Drama	rec.art.theater.plays	Theater and drama
Food and drink	rec.crafts.brewing rec.food.historic alt.food.ice-cream	Beer brewing History of food Ice cream
Fun	alt.religion.santaism	Santa Claus
Games	alt.atari-jaguar.discussion rec.games.video.nintendo	Video games Nintendo video games
Government	clari.news.usa.gov.white_house	White House news
Health	alt.support.diet clari.tw.health	Dieting support Health care and medicine
Hobbies	rec.radio.amateur.equipment rec.antiques rec.juggling rec.crafts.quilting	Equipment for amateur radios Buy, sell, and trade antiques Juggling oranges, numbers, etc. Quilting
Home	alt.home.repair alt.hoovers	Home repair Vacuum cleaners
Humor	alt.humor.puns	Word play
Jobs	bionet.jobs.wanted misc.jobs.offered.entry misc.jobs.resumes	Biological sciences jobs Entry-level jobs Posted resumes
Medicine	alt.med.allergy sci.med.dentistry	Causes and treatments for allergies Dentistry
Music	rec.music.classical rec.music.marketplace rec.music.compose	Classical music Buy or sell musical instruments, equipment, records, etc. Compose original music
Pets	alt.aquaria rec.equestrian rec.pets.birds rec.pets.cats rec.pets.dogs	Tropical fish Horse lovers Advice and anecdotes on birds Advice and anecdotes on cats Advice and anecdotes on dogs
Science	sci.astro.planetarium bionet.cellbiol alt.energy.renewable	Planetarium programs Cell biology Renewable energy

3 Finding Resources Using Gopher

INTRODUCTION

The Internet takes you to computers that are jammed with information. The problem is how to quickly find the information you are interested in. One of the tools used to "surf the net" is Gopher. In this lab you will learn how to use it to find information on a wide range of topics and to download files from other computers to your computer.

Additionally, you will learn how to link directly to other computers using Telnet.

About Gopher

Gopher is a software program that allows you to easily access a variety of resources on the Internet. More specifically, it is a program that integrates a variety of services into a single application, thereby making it easy to navigate and use many of the Internet services and systems. Gopher provides a menu-based interface that allows you to search, retrieve, and display documents from remote sites. Some of the types of information you can get using Gopher include: newspaper articles, movie reviews, weather forecasts, e-mail addresses and phone books, journals, and so on.

Gopher uses a client-server model in which the client and server are two computer programs that communicate with each other. To use Gopher you run a Gopher **client program** on your computer. The client interprets the user's keystrokes and commands and connects via the Internet to a Gopher server program. A Gopher **server program** is on a computer at a remote site that accesses a database of file lists and information on that computer. There are several thousand Gopher servers on the Internet today, with the number increasing all the time. The computers that are Gopher servers run 24 hours a day, waiting for requests from client programs for information. The client then displays the server's resources through a series of menus.

Competencies

After completing this lab, you will know how to:

1. Select Gopher menus.
2. Use the history list.
3. Create a bookmark.
4. Search gopherspace.
5. Download files.
6. Make a Telnet connection.
7. Use white pages.

Gopher was developed at the University of Minnesota in 1991 and was named after the school's mascot.

INTERNET

The information you can access through Gopher may be on your host computer (the server the client initially contacts) or on a different computer on the other side of the world. The space that contains the menus and information you can access using Gopher is called **gopherspace**. Gopherspace has a tree-like structure. The root (home) server is where you begin your search for information. As you go up the tree, branches of menus shoot off from the main trunk to other sources, and so on. The tree is well organized by subject matter, making the search logical and easy.

Gopher automatically handles all commands needed to connect to another computer and makes it easy to download files to your computer. While using Gopher you are connected to the server for only the time it takes to load the menus or download the file. This minimizes the amount of time you use the Internet and consequently saves network resources.

Some Gopher clients use a Windows interface that includes mouse support and icons. Others are character-based and consist of simple lists of menus. This book assumes the use of a Windows-based Gopher client called HGopher. The style of other Gophers is similar to the Windows-based HGopher so the instructions will easily translate.

Selecting Gopher Menus

Load Windows and open the program group that contains HGopher. (Some examples of the program group name where this application may be located are Winsock, Internet for Windows, or Net Tools.)

To start the Gopher client program and begin a search,

Double-click:

Your screen will look similar to Figure 3-1, although it will reflect items specific to your school.

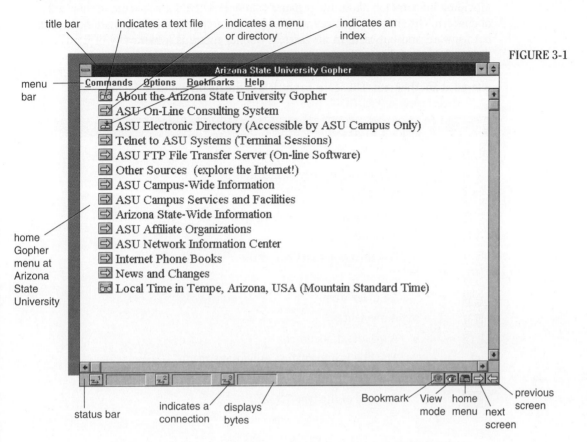

FIGURE 3-1

title bar   indicates a text file   indicates a menu   indicates an
or directory   index

menu bar

home Gopher menu at Arizona State University

status bar   indicates a   displays
connection   bytes

Bookmark   View   home   next   previous
mode   menu   screen   screen

The client program automatically connects to the client or host Gopher server, and the opening Gopher window is displayed. Below the menu bar is the directory menu for the host Gopher server. This is called the **home** or **root Gopher menu**. It is the top-level menu. The menu you see on your screen will be similar to that shown in Figure 3-1, although the wording and order of menu items will be different. The way information is presented on a menu is determined by the client software. The client software takes the server's menu and displays it in its own fashion.

INTERNET

Gopher menus are designed to match the needs of users and organizations. Therefore, many different approaches are used in Gopher menus. Some lead inward, providing information about the organization only. Others are specific to their areas of concern. Others are organized around types of activities and information, leading both inward and outward. In all cases, a Gopher menu is a hierarchy of items and directories, much like a file system.

The menu items may refer to another menu, a file, a file search, or a service offered at another site. The icons to the left of the menu indicate the following:

Icon	Represents
	A gopher directory or menu
	Previous directory or menu
	A text item
	A file item
	A sound item
	A connection to a CSO server
	A graphic image item
	An index item
	A movie item
	A hypertext document
	The line is information only (not a menu)
	A Telnet item
	An item of the type TN3270

The status bar is the bottom line of the screen. The left end of the status bar displays three buttons and boxes. The ⊞ button indicates that a connection is being made and the box displays the number of bytes being transferred. Clicking on the button while a transfer is in progress will cancel the transfer.

The icons on the right end of the status bar have the following meanings:

Icon	Meaning
	Displays the Bookmark menu
	Indicates you are in View mode—clicking on it displays text file for viewing
	Indicates you are in Copy to File mode—clicking on it saves file to a directory and name you specify
	Indicates you are in Copy to Directory mode—clicking on it saves file automatically to Windows directory
	Returns you to home menu
	Next or previous screen of information

Selecting a menu takes you to another directory, opens an application, or establishes a direct computer connection. To select a menu, double-click on the item.

Select a menu item that is preceded with a ⇨ and whose topic area indicates that it will provide information about your school (college, admissions, campus events, and so on) or your community.

The first box on the left end of the status bar displays the number of bytes as the client accesses the information on the server. If response time is very fast, you may not see any information appear in the box. If this area displays Connect or 0 and does not change for a while, this indicates the system is slow. The title bar displays "Getting Requested Item" to tell you the retrieval of your request is still in progress. You may have to wait a few moments.

Sometimes certain documents or connections take a long time to show up on your screen. There are several reasons for this. You may be accessing several different servers to get the information. Some servers are very popular and thus are overloaded with requests, making response time slow. Other times the server may be temporarily down. However, you may find an alternate route to the same information through many different "tunnels" in gopherspace.

Do not click on the icon in front of the menu item. This will give you information on the menu only.

INTERNET

Your screen should be similar to Figure 3-2.

Your screen will reflect menu
items at your school.

selected menu item
on previous menu

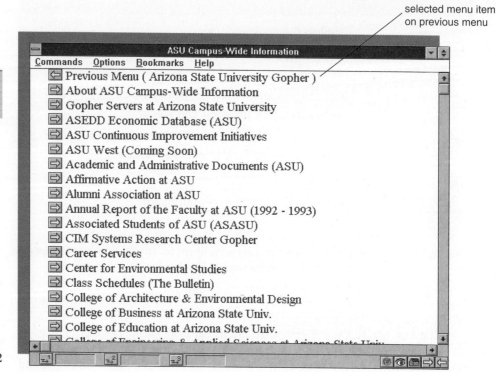

FIGURE 3-2

Another menu of topics related to the topic area you selected appears. You are one
menu level below the home menu. When a menu item is selected, if it points to
another menu, the client connects to the server and retrieves the menu. Then the
client disconnects from the server and waits for your next request. It has, however,
remembered where it was so it can return and go further or move in another
direction. This makes connection time to the server very short (fractions of a second).

Notice that the first menu option now is Previous Menu followed by the title of
the menu you were last in. Clicking on this first menu item will return you to the
menu you were last viewing.

Next you will view a text file. Menu options preceded by the eyeglasses icon
indicate that the item is a text file.

If this menu contains an item preceded with , select it. If it does not,
continue to select other menu options until you find a menu that has an item that is
preceded with this symbol, and then select it.

As the file is loaded, the status bar displays its progress in bytes. Next the text
viewer program is loaded and the document is displayed in the viewer window. A
viewer program is a separate program that is designed to display different types of
files. Gopher automatically loads the viewer program when it is needed to display
text files.

The text viewer program
must already be installed on
your computer system.

Your screen should be similar to Figure 3-3.

selected menu   selected text file displayed
                                                 in text viewer window

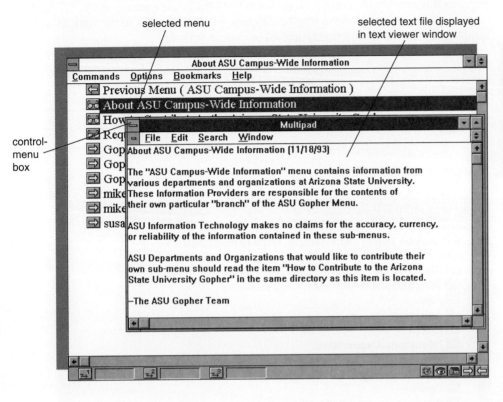

The document you are viewing will display different information than in Figure 3-3.

Multipad is the text viewer application used in this example.

control-menu box

FIGURE 3-3

Read the entire document.
    To close the viewer application,

Choose: File>Exit
or
Double-click: viewer window control-menu box

The Gopher menu you were last in is available for selections again.
    To quickly return to your home Gopher menu,

If necessary, scroll the window to see the rest of the text.

You can move and size the viewer window like any other Windows application.

Choose: Commands>Go Home
or
Click: Home

    So far you have used menus that have accessed information at your host Gopher server. Now you will move out onto the Internet to access information from other sites.
    Another type of information you can view using Gopher are graphic images such as pictures. You have heard that the University of Illinois has a computer that provides hourly weather satellite images. To access this location, you will need to select the menu option from your home menu that will take you to other Gopher and information servers. The menu option (shown in Figure 3-1) that leads to this menu is "Other Sources (explore the Internet!)." Selecting this menu will display another menu containing an option such as Other Gopher and Information Servers.

INTERNET

This wording may be different on different servers, and it may appear on the home menu as it is here, or on a menu a level down from the home menu.

Since your Gopher menu may be different, fill in the spaces to the right of our sample with the menu selections supplied by your instructor.

Selections from your school's Gopher menu

Select: Other Sources (explore the Internet!) _____

Select: Other Gopher and Information Servers _____

_____

Your screen should be similar to Figure 3-4.

FIGURE 3-4

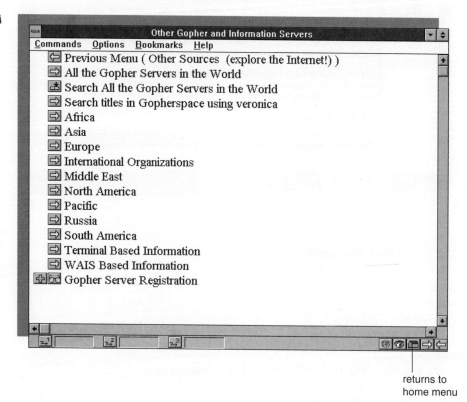

returns to
home menu

To locate the weather satellite images, you will navigate geographically through gopherspace. Since the images are located at the University of Illinois weather machine computer, to get to this location,

Select: North America
Select: USA

You are now many levels into gopherspace below your home Gopher menu. This menu lists each state in the United States. Before moving to Illinois, to see a list of Gopher servers in your state,

Select: your state (or another state of your choice other than Illinois)

View the menu of Gopher servers available in your state.

To continue to a Gopher server in Illinois, you need to return to the previous menu and select Illinois.

Select: Previous Menu (USA)

or

Click: 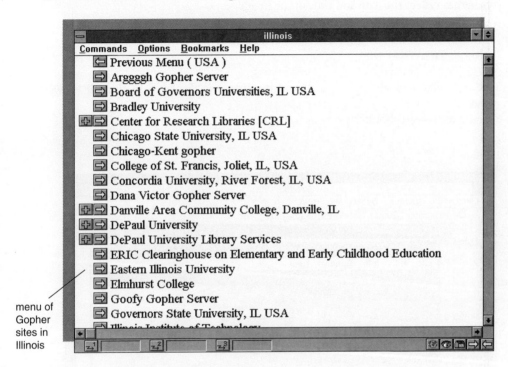 Previous screen

Select: Illinois

Your screen should be similar to Figure 3-5.

FIGURE 3-5

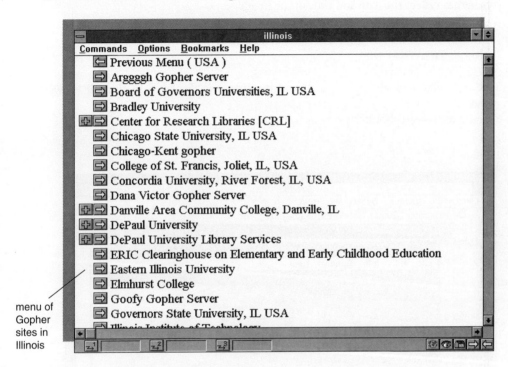

menu of
Gopher
sites in
Illinois

You are now viewing a menu of Gopher servers in Illinois. To access the Gopher server where the weather satellite images are located,

Select: University of Illinois weather machine

Note: If the weather machine is busy, try reselecting the menu item. If it continues to be busy, try to view an alternate weather image by making the following selections: University of Chicago>World News & Weather>Weather and Weather Services Satellite Maps (via UMN)>Weather Services Satellite Maps>Weather Photo of North America (Infrared). Your weather image will be similar to Figure 3-6. If this is unsuccessful, read the rest of this section and continue at "Using the History List." Try accessing the weather machine at a later time.

> You will need to scroll the menu to locate the University of Illinois weather machine menu.

The home Gopher menu for the University of Illinois weather machine computer is displayed. To move to the directory containing the weather satellite images,

Select: Images
Select: Satellite Images
Select: Satellite USIR

You are now at least eight menu levels from your home Gopher menu. This menu displays a list of file names all ending with the .GIF file extension. **GIF** (Graphic Interchange Format) file extensions indicate graphic image files. The camera icon ▣ preceding the file name also indicates that the file type is a graphic image. The file names reflect the date and time of the image.

To see the most recent satellite image,

Select: 00LATEST.GIF

The GIF viewer program is loaded and the image is displayed in the GIF viewer window.

Your screen should be similar to Figure 3-6.

> To view GIF images, a GIF viewer program must already be installed on your computer system.

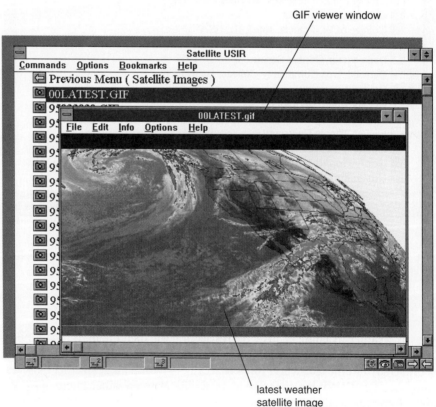

GIF viewer window

latest weather
satellite image

FIGURE 3-6

An infrared map of the current U.S. weather image is displayed in the GIF viewer window. If you want, you can scroll the image in the window to better view different areas. When you have finished viewing the file, you can continue your search for other information.

To exit the viewer program and close the window,

Choose: File>Exit

or

Double-click: GIF window's control-menu box

If you want, select other GIF files and view the images. Close the GIF window when you are done.

Using the History List

Your location in gopherspace is far from your home Gopher menu. Sometimes you may want to review the menu selections you have made so far. To see this list of selections, called a **history list**,

Choose: Commands>History

Your screen should be similar to Figure 3-7.

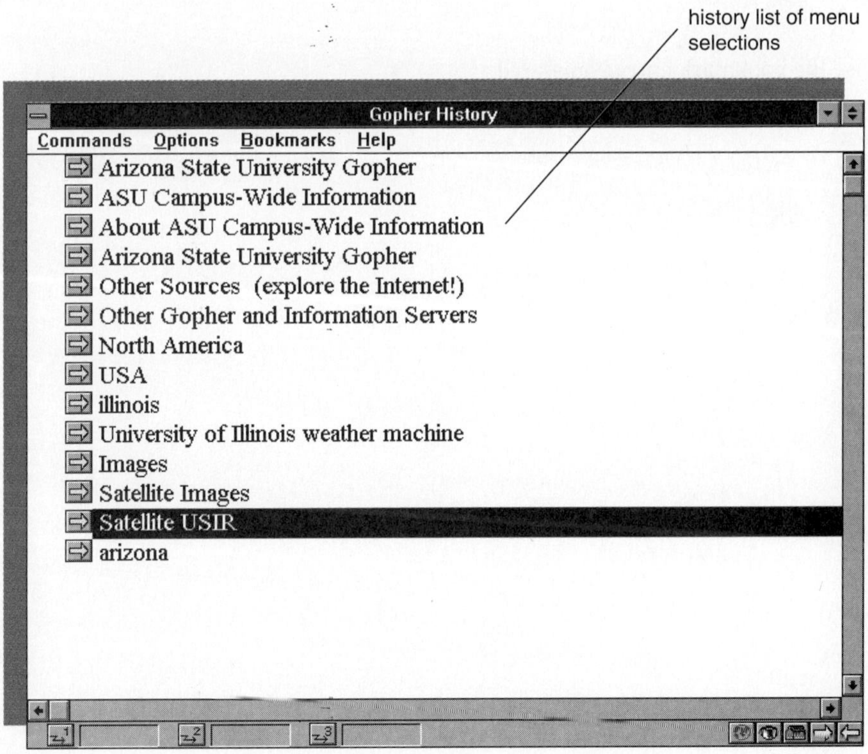

history list of menu
selections

FIGURE 3-7

The Gopher History window displays your menu selections. The history list displays a direct path to the selected item followed by any other paths you may have selected. In addition to viewing where you have been, you can select from this list to quickly move back to a previously viewed item. As you can see, you are many steps from the home Gopher menu.

To return to your current location,

Double-click: Satellite USIR (or the item you were last on)

Creating a Bookmark

If you wanted to return to this location in the future, it would take many selections and a good memory. When you find places that you would like to return to later, you can mark the location using a Gopher **bookmark**. You can create a bookmark to any menu or file. You would like to create a bookmark for the 00LATEST.GIF file.

Highlight the 00LATEST.GIF file name (or the last menu you accessed).

> Use the Mark Menu option if your current selection is a menu instead of a file.

Choose: Bookmarks>Mark Item

Next you will return to your home Gopher menu and try using the bookmark. To quickly return to your home Gopher menu,

Click: 🔲 Home

To view the bookmark entry you stored,

Choose: Bookmarks>Show Bookmarks
or
Click: 🔲 Bookmarks

Your screen should be similar to Figure 3-8.

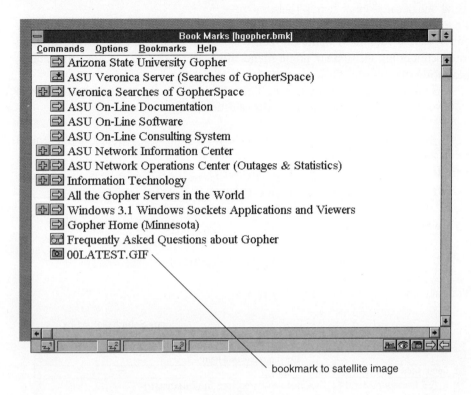

bookmark to satellite image

FIGURE 3-8

The screen displays the bookmark you saved.

To return to the weather image file,

Select: 00LATEST.GIF (or the location you saved)

You have quickly jumped to the specified location.

If you were unable to access the weather machine earlier to view the satellite image, return to the section above and complete the selections needed to view the image.

Close the weather image file and return to your home Gopher menu.

Searching Gopherspace

As you can see, searching through so many levels in gopherspace can take a lot of time before you locate what you are interested in. For example, if you did not know the location of the weather images, they would have been very difficult to find using

> If you get an error message and the map does not open, try the command again. Sometimes when you use bookmarks to jump to a specific location, the program may be unable to locate the marked item and trying the command again usually works.

INTERNET

this method. If you know what you are looking for, you can locate it more quickly using one of the Gopher search tools.

The menu option "Search All the Gopher Servers in the World" is a menu option that is commonly found on many Gopher servers. This option will search an index containing all Gopher home menu titles. The 📥 icon precedes this menu, indicating that the entry leads to an index.

Since your Gopher menu may be different, substitute the appropriate selection(s) from your school's Gopher menu for the selections below.

Selections from your school's Gopher menu

Select: Other Sources (explore the Internet!) _____
Select: Other Gopher and Information Servers _____

To use this index to search,

Select: Search All the Gopher Servers in the World

Your screen should be similar to Figure 3-9.

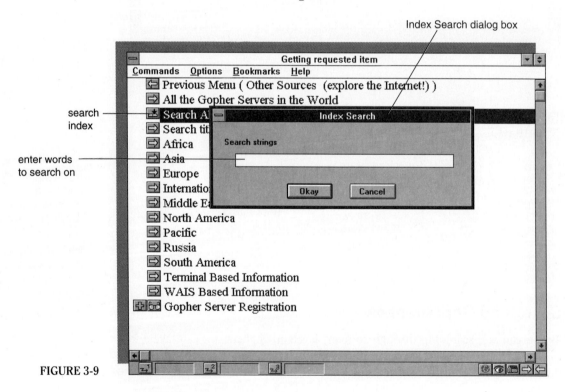

FIGURE 3-9

An Index Search dialog box appears. In the entry space, you enter the words you want the search to locate. To see how quickly you may be able to locate the weather Gopher server,

Type: weather
Choose: Okay

You could press ⏎Enter to choose Okay.

After a few minutes, your screen should be similar to Figure 3-10.

menus located using
search of Gopher servers

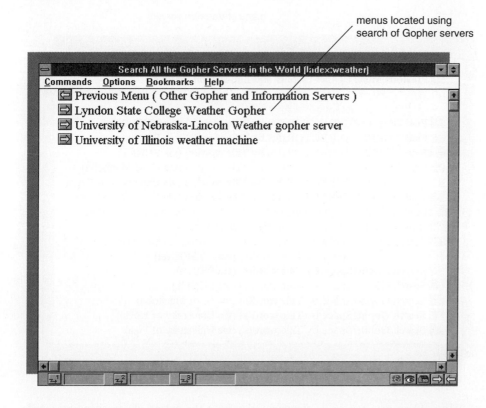

FIGURE 3-10

Several matches were found that contained the word "weather" in Gopher home menus. The University of Illinois weather machine is one of the matches. Selecting this item would take you to the Gopher menu at this site. From there, however, you would still need to explore menus to locate the satellite images.

Return to the previous menu.

Another search tool called **Veronica** assists you in finding information in gopherspace by searching for word matches in titles and menus. Veronica maintains an index of about 15 million items from about 5,500 Gopher servers. The index is updated about once a month. When using Veronica, you enter search words and Veronica looks through index titles to find matching words. You will use Veronica to locate weather satellite images.

Veronica stands for "very easy rodent-oriented net-wide index of computerized archives."

Substitute the appropriate selection(s) from your school's Gopher menu for the solution below.

Selections from your school's Gopher menu

Select: Search titles in Gopherspace using Veronica _____

_____

_____

Your screen should be similar to Figure 3-11.

menu of Veronica servers

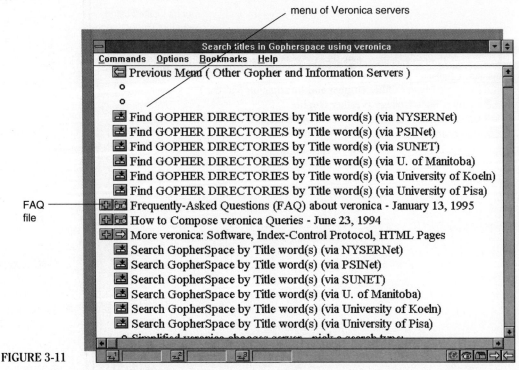

FIGURE 3-11

FAQ
file

A menu of Veronica servers is displayed. You have the option of searching for words in menu names (directories) or in menu items (title words) using any of the Veronica servers. It does not matter which server you select, because they should all produce the same results. However, some servers may be updated more recently than others, thereby providing more up-to-date matches. Moreover, some are more heavily used, making them slower.

If your Gopher menu now includes a Simplified Veronica menu option, selecting this option will contact all Veronica servers for you, saving you from trying servers until you find one that is not busy.

You will search directories for the words "weather" and "machine."

> Read the Veronica FAQ text file for more information about using Veronica.

Select: Find GOPHER DIRECTORIES by Title word(s) (via University of Pisa)

Your screen should be similar to Figure 3-12.

enter words to search on

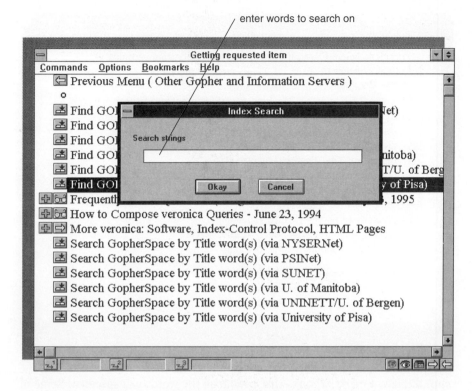

FIGURE 3-12

A dialog box appears in which you enter the text you want Veronica to locate. To locate all titles that include the words "weather" and "machine,"

Type: weather machine
Choose: Okay

The search is not case-sensitive, so you can enter the words in either upper-case or lowercase.

The dialog box may already contain the word "weather" from your previous search.

INTERNET

Your screen should be similar to Figure 3-13.

menus
containing
matches
to your
search

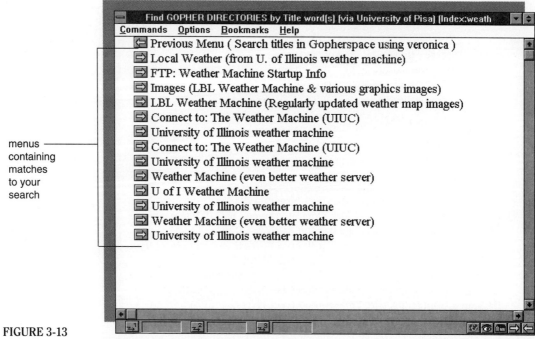

FIGURE 3-13

Veronica displays a menu of items that contained the words you specified. Some of the menu items may be duplicates. If necessary, scroll the list until you locate the University of Illinois weather machine.

Using Veronica is a beginning to finding information. If you carefully select the words to search on, you can help narrow the number of items that will be located. For example, the search you just conducted used multiple words, "weather machine." Only those items with both words were located, making the search scope quite specific. A search on "weather machine" may find 60 matches, while a search on "weather" may find thousands of matches. The search words do not need to be in the order in which they may appear in the title, but the words must be at least two characters long. Generally, by default the first 200 matches are displayed.

Downloading Files

The Internet makes available a huge number of files at computers throughout the world. Many times, rather than viewing the file onscreen while using Internet, you may want to look at it later. Many of these files are software applications, graphic images, or large text files that are freely available for you to transfer from the remote computer to your computer. The process of copying a file to your computer from a remote site is called **downloading**. Then you can access the files using the appropriate software program. FTP or File Transfer Protocol is a way to download files of software, text, and graphics from the Internet. This feature is built into the Gopher system.

You would like to find biographical information about the current Supreme Court justices and download this information to your computer.

Use Veronica to locate sources on Supreme Court justices. If necessary, select a menu that indicates it contains biographical information. Select one of the items from the list that is a text file (preceded with 📄). If this source does not provide biographical information on one or all the justices, close it and select others until you find one that has this information. When you are done reading the information, close the text viewer.

> You may need to select different menu items before you find the menu that contains the biographical information on the justices.

Next you want to download a copy of this file to your computer. By default, when you first start Gopher, the 🔘 icon appears in the status bar. This indicates that when you select a file, it will be displayed onscreen by a viewer. If you click on this icon, it switches first to a 🗀 icon, and then to a 🖼 icon.

Click: 🔘 View file

The icon changes to 🗀. This indicates that when the item is selected, you will be able to copy the file to the location you specify.

Click: 🗀 Copy to file

Now the icon appears as 🖼. This indicates that when you select a file, it will be copied and saved directly to the Windows directory of your hard disk.

To copy the file to a location you specify, display the 🗀 icon.

Double-click: the Supreme Court justices biographical information file you selected

Your screen should be similar to Figure 3-14.

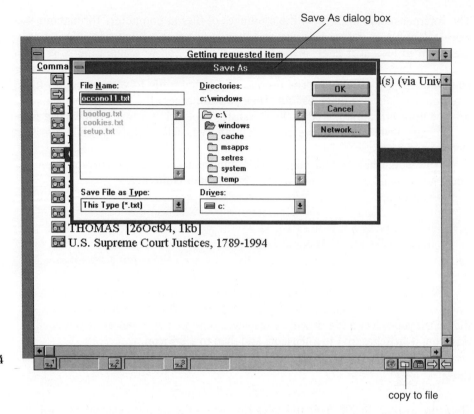

FIGURE 3-14

A Save As dialog box appears. This box is like most other Windows Save As dialog boxes, in that it allows you to specify a file name and to select a drive and directory to save the file to. You will save the file as JUSTICES.TXT on a floppy disk.

Insert a disk in the appropriate drive for your system.

In the File Name text box,

Type: **justices.txt**

Specify the appropriate drive and path for your setup.

Choose: OK

The status bar indicates that the transfer is in progress and when it is completed. At a later time, you can open this file using any word processor.

To change the button back to allow viewing of files, change the ⬜ icon to 👁. Return to your home Gopher menu.

Making a Telnet Connection

Through Gopher you can also communicate directly to other computers on the Internet using Telnet. **Telnet** is an application that allows you to log on and communicate from your local personal computer to a remote computer. After logging on to a remote computer, you can run programs on that computer by typing single-line commands or by selecting from a menu.

You will use Telnet to communicate with the NASA Spacelink computer whose target audience is teachers and students. It provides information on space missions, educational programs, and scientific projects.

Perform a Veronica search on NASA Spacelink. If you get a menu of NASA Spacelinks without Telnet icons, select menu options until you do. Locate a NASA Spacelink menu item with a Telnet icon (usually at the bottom of the list). Select the Telnet NASA Spacelink menu item.

The connection is made. You may also receive a warning message indicating that you are leaving Gopher and connecting directly with another computer.

If you cannot establish a Telnet connection, return to your home Gopher menu. Read the rest of this section for information about this procedure. Continue with the section "Using White Pages."

Your screen should be similar to Figure 3-15.

> Telnet menu items are preceded with the 🖥 or 🖳 icon.

> Your computer must have the appropriate Telnet software installed in order to establish a connection.

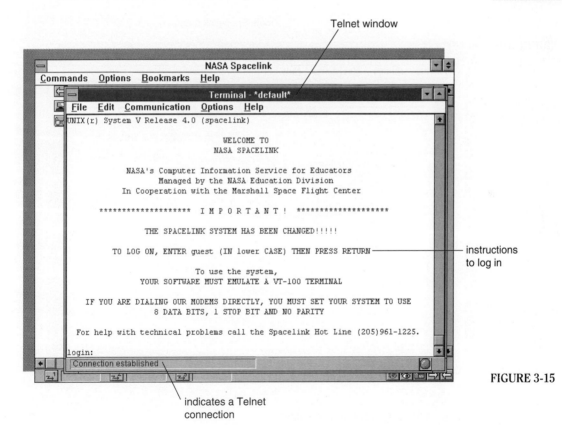

Telnet window

instructions to log in

indicates a Telnet connection

FIGURE 3-15

Note: You may reach a different NASA Spacelink location than the one shown in Figure 3-15. You can either read and follow the instructions as they appear on your screen, or select another NASA Spacelink until you find the one displayed here, then follow the instructions below.

You are now communicating directly with another computer and have established a constant connection to this computer.

The NASA Spacelink welcome window appears advising you of the login access word. Following the instructions on the screen, to enter the login password,

Some Telnet sessions do not require a log-in password.

Type: guest
Press: ⏎Enter

The password is accepted and an important message screen appears. Read this information. When you are ready to continue,

Press: ⏎Enter

Your screen should be similar to Figure 3-16.

main Spacelink menu

FIGURE 3-16

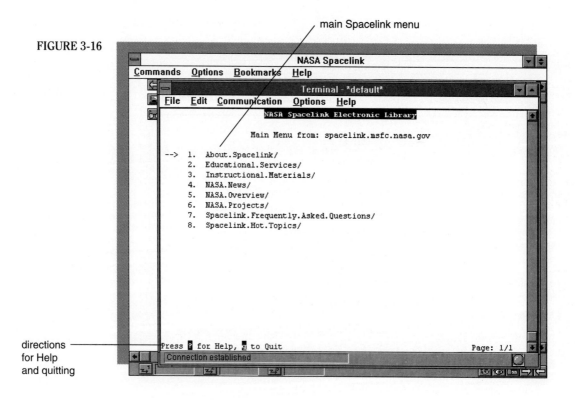

directions
for Help
and quitting

The main Spacelink menu is displayed.

You will find that different locations you Telnet to have different appearances and different procedures. Usually, there is a Help command that provides instructions on basic navigational procedures and directions on how to exit the Telnet session.

You will use the menu to find out more information on NASA. To select a menu item, you can type the menu line number and press ⌐⏎Enter⌐ or move the highlight to the line and then press ⌐⏎Enter⌐.

Select: 4. NASA.News/

A new menu of choices is displayed. To find out more information on launch dates and payloads,

Select: 1. Launch.Dates.and.Payloads/

A third menu of items is displayed. To see the actual manifests, select the currently displayed fleet manifest menu option.

When you are done reading the information on your screen,

Type: u

You are returned to the previous menu. You can use the U (Up) command to move up through all the menus you have selected.

Select other menu items to see what type of information they contain.

When you are done exploring the Spacelink menus, to quit the Telnet session,

Type: Q

A prompt asking if you really want to quit is displayed. To confirm your request,

Type: Y

You are disconnected from the NASA Spacelink computer.

Close the Telnet window and return to your home Gopher menu.

Using White Pages

Another resource available through Gopher is a database commonly called the **white pages**. It is used to search for e-mail addresses or names. The Internet has several different types of white pages services. Access to white pages through Gopher is generally from a menu called Phone Books or White Pages.

Since your Gopher menu will be different, fill in the spaces to the right of the sample with the menu selections supplied by your instructor.

Selections from your school's Gopher menu

Select: Internet Phone Books _____

_____

> If this is no longer on the menu, select another item.

> Do not select picture items because your system may not be set up to receive the files.

Your screen should be similar to Figure 3-17.

FIGURE 3-17

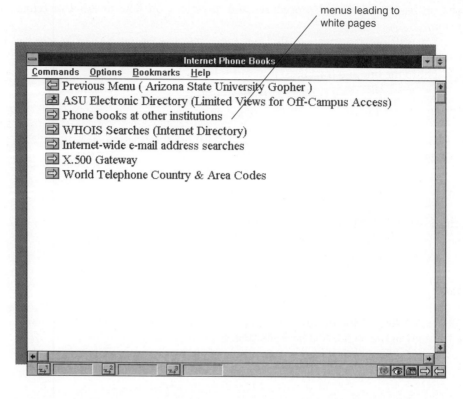

menus leading to
white pages

The phonebook submenu generally displays several menus of white pages directories. To demonstrate using the white pages, you will search for a person whose last name is Brown and who is employed at a campus of the University of California system. Commonly, the phonebook submenu will include a menu for phone books at other institutions, which will take you to other menus of phone books.

Select: Phone books at other institutions

To continue to navigate the menus to narrow the geographical location of white pages,

Select: North American

A list of organizations appears. The icon indicates the organization uses a CSO (Computing Services Organization) style server, and ▣ indicates a Gopher index server. The CSO style servers display a screen in which you enter the search information. The more specific the information, the narrower the search results. A Gopher index server displays a dialog box similar to the Veronica dialog box in which you enter the search value, such as the name.

Select: University of California at Davis

A search dialog box appears in which you enter the person's name.

Type: Brown
Choose: Do Query

Your screen should be similar to Figure 3-18.

search on name of Brown   results of search

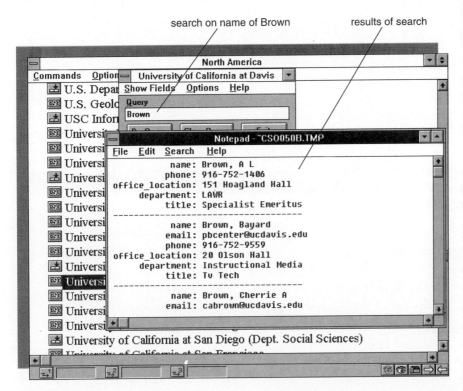

FIGURE 3-18

A list of all matches is displayed. E-mail addresses are included if they are available. The type of output displayed depends upon the information made available at the organization.

Close the text viewer and search dialog boxes. Return to your home Gopher menu.

To exit Gopher,

Choose: Commands>Exit
or
Double-click: control-menu box

When you exit, you will be prompted to save your bookmark. On your own computer system, you would probably want to save the bookmark. However, since you are using a school computer, you will not save the bookmark.

Select: No

The Windows program group is displayed.

Key Terms

Gopher   (IN81)
client program   (IN81)
server program   (IN81)
gopherspace   (IN82)
home Gopher menu   (IN83)
root Gopher menu   (IN83)
GIF   (IN90)
history list   (IN91)
bookmark   (IN92)
Veronica   (IN95)
download   (IN99)
Telnet   (IN101)
white pages   (IN103)

Command Summary

HGopher Command	Icon	Action
Commands>**G**o Home		Returns to Gopher home menu
Commands>**H**istory		Displays a list of selections you have made
Bookmarks>**M**ark Item		Marks an item location
Bookmarks>Show **B**ookmark		Shows all marked locations
Commands>**E**xit		Exits Gopher

Matching

1. gopherspace   _____   **a.** marked location in gopherspace

2. home menu   _____   **b.** icon for text file

3.   _____   **c.** file extension for graphic image file

4. Telnet   _____   **d.** menus and information you can access with Gopher

5. Gopher   _____   **e.** transfers file to your own computer

6. history list   _____   **f.** search program

7. bookmark   _____   **g.** list of menus or commands you have used

8. FTP   _____   **h.** top-level menu of server

9.   _____   **i.** connect to another computer through Gopher

10. .GIF   _____   **j.** icon for image item

Short-Answer Questions

1. What is Gopher?
2. What is a server?
3. What is the difference between a Gopher client and a Gopher server?
4. How do you make selections on a Gopher menu?
5. Explain the advantages of using a Gopher.
6. What is Veronica?
7. How can you narrow searches using Veronica?
8. How can you find someone's e-mail address using Gopher?
9. What is FTP?
10. What does Telnet allow you to do?

Practice Exercises

1. Justin is doing a report on the U.S. Senate. He would like to use Gopher to find out what types of questions people ask about the Senate. Using the following menu selections as a guide, try to find the FAQs for the U.S. Senate.

   Other Sources (explore the Internet!)
   US Govt/Agencies Info
   Govt Info
   Fed Info
   US Senate

2. Why would you want to browse a library you cannot physically visit? Many libraries share books, so if yours does not have what you want, you can tell the librarian where to get it. Or if you live in an area where the libraries are not yet on-line, you can use Telnet to do some basic bibliographic research before you go to your local branch. Several hundred libraries around the world, including the Library of Congress, are now available to you through Telnet. In this exercise you will make a Telnet connection to a library and search for books and information on computer crime.

   a. Use the Gopher menu selections listed below as a guide to make a Telnet connection to the University of Minnesota Library.

   Other Sources (explore the Internet!)

   Libraries

   University of Minnesota Libraries

   University of Minnesota Libraries, University of Minnesota

   LUMINA terminal session (your instructor will provide you with the correct terminal session)

b. You are now connected to the Lumina Telnet session of the University of Minnesota Library. To connect to the library's catalog, choose the following two menu selections.

University Library/Lumina

MNCAT

c. Follow the instructions for searching for subjects at the library to locate information on computer crime. (The command "S=computer crime" would be appropriate.)

d. Follow the instructions for more complete information on a listing of your choice. Write down the titles of three sources you located.

e. Quit your Telnet session and return to the home Gopher menu.

Although you cannot borrow books from the library, the search may lead to books that you can ask your local library to locate or, if they participate in a library exchange, request for you.

3. Use Veronica to search for the NASA space calendar of events. What steps did you use to locate the file? Download the space calendar to your disk.

4. Thousands of searches are possible using Veronica. Try some of the searches suggested below and then try some of your own. Download at least two files you locate to your floppy disk. If you already know how to use a word processing program, open and print the files.

a. Do you want to find museums that have images of artwork from their exhibits on display? Try searching for "museum" using Veronica.

b. Are you looking for a copy of the Declaration of Independence? Try "declaration."

c. Do you want copies of Environmental Protection Agency fact sheets on hundreds of chemicals? Try "education" and "environmental fact sheets."

d. Do you want to know when your favorite team is playing again? Look up schedules for teams in various professional sports leagues by searching for "professional sports schedules."

e. Look up weather forecasts for North America or bone up on your weather facts.

5. You are planning to rent a movie at the local video store. Instead of wandering around reading all the boxes, you would like to use Gopher to locate movie reviews before you go.

   a. Using the following menu selections as a guide, locate the movie review for the movie "Manhattan Murder Mystery."

   U of Minn

   Fun & Games

   Movie Reviews

   Current USENET movie reviews

   1993

   Sept

   b. Use the History command and return to the Current USENET movie reviews menu and search for other movies you may be interested in. Download a movie review file to your floppy disk. If you already know how to use a word processing program, open and print the file.

6. You are preparing a paper for a course in your field of study.

   a. Use Gopher and/or Veronica to locate three text files that contain information on the topic of your paper.

   b. Write down the text file names as they appear in the menu and write a brief summary of the information in the text files. (Remember, you can download the files to your disk. Check the size of the file before you download it to ensure that you have enough disk space.)

Browsing the World Wide Web

4

INTRODUCTION

The newest source of information on the Internet is the World Wide Web (WWW). The WWW allows users to quickly jump from one information source to another related source. These sources of information may be on the same computer or different computers around the world. In this lab you will explore the WWW using the Netscape and Yahoo programs.

About the World Wide Web

The **World Wide Web** consists of information organized into **pages** containing text and graphic images. But most importantly, a page contains **hypertext links**, or highlighted keywords and images, that lead to related information. Clicking on the links quickly transports you to the location where that information is stored. The links may take you to other pages, text files, graphic images, movies, or audio clips. The Web allows users to view millions of pages of information by jumping from one related source to another through the links.

To access the WWW, you must have a browser software program. **Browsers** display text and images, access FTP sites, and provide in one tool an uncomplicated interface to the Internet and WWW documents. In contrast to Gopher, which needs separate viewer software to display graphics, movies, and text, browser programs include this software, making all types of information on the Internet very accessible. Browsers allow you to surf the net unencumbered by the complexity of how to access information on the Internet. However, because the WWW is fairly new, only a limited amount of information on the Internet can be accessed at present through the WWW. Therefore, it is still important to know how to use Gopher and to understand FTP and Telnet.

Competencies

After completing this lab, you will know how to:

1. Use Netscape.
2. Select links.
3. Use Yahoo.
4. Use the URL.
5. Read newsgroups using Netscape.
6. Send e-mail through Netscape.

CERN (the Center for European Nuclear Research in Switzerland) designed and developed the WWW system.

INTERNET

Three popular browser programs are Lynx, Mosaic, and Netscape. The Lynx program does not display graphic images, but allows you to use hypertext links to move to pages. Mosaic and **Netscape** run under Windows and provide a complete graphical interface to the Web. Most of the Internet commands are hidden behind buttons, pictures, and underlined words and phrases that you click on to access. This lab will use the Netscape browser to explore the WWW.

Exploring the Netscape Window

Load Windows and open the program group containing the Netscape program.

> Your instructor will tell you the name of the program group containing the Netscape application.

Some examples of the program group names where this application may be located are Winsock, Internet for Windows, or Net Tools.

To begin Netscape,

> Some Web sites may briefly display a welcome page before the home page.

Double-click:

Your screen should be similar to Figure 4-1.

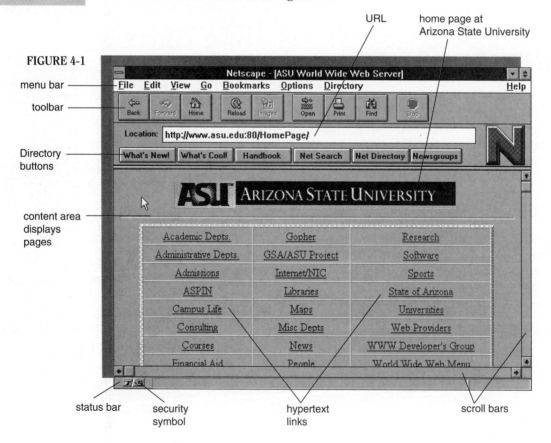

FIGURE 4-1

menu bar
toolbar
Directory buttons
content area displays pages
status bar
security symbol
hypertext links
scroll bars
URL
home page at Arizona State University

The Netscape program is loaded and displays your school's home page. The **home page** is the page that the Netscape program has been set to load by default. Each home page is designed by the people at the WWW site and will contain different information. However, there are similarities between home pages. Generally, home pages include a brief welcome with information about the site and a menu. Probably the first thing you will notice about the page is the highlighted (underlined or colored) text. This indicates a hypertext link.

As in other Windows applications, the Netscape window has a title bar, control-menu boxes, minimize and maximize/restore buttons, scroll bars, a menu bar, and a toolbar. Pull-down menu items activate the same features as toolbar buttons plus many additional features that are less frequently used.

The menus offer Netscape options that allow you to control the screen appearance and how Netscape performs, as well as provide Help information and general file utilities such as saving and printing. In addition, you can use menus to create bookmarks to pages and see a history list of pages that you have viewed in the current session.

The toolbar buttons activate the Netscape features most commonly used. The toolbar buttons are described below.

Button	Action
Back	Returns to previous page viewed
Forward	Displays next page after using Back
Home	Displays home page
Reload	Accesses and redisplays document you are viewing
Images	Loads only images in current document
Open	Displays a dialog box to move to a specific page
Print	Prints the active document
Find	Searches text of current document for specified text
Stop	Interrupts transfer of incoming data

If you are using a different version of Netscape, your buttons may be slightly different.

Below the toolbar buttons is another set of buttons called the Directory buttons. **Directory buttons** display pages containing information to help you browse the Internet. These buttons are described below.

Button	Action
What's New!	Displays Netscape's list of selected new topics
What's Cool!	Displays Netscape's list of selected popular topics
Handbook	Displays information on how to use Netscape
Net Search	Displays list of Internet search tools
Net Directory	Displays master directory of other Internet directories
Newsgroups	Accesses newsgroups

If you are using a different version of Netscape, your buttons may be slightly different.

The large center area of the window is the **content area**. This area displays pages and other information sources you have accessed. Currently it displays the home page. As you link to other sources, the content area displays the page associated with the requested link. The vertical and horizontal scroll bars can be used to scroll the text in the content area.

Each page has a unique web identifier called a **URL** (Uniform Resource Locator). The URL provides location information that is used to navigate through the Internet to access a page. The URL for the page you are viewing is displayed in the Location field. Generally, you do not need to know the page's URL to get to it. This is because the hypertext link contains the URL and automatically makes the connection for you when you click on it. Sometimes you will not have an automatic link to a page, in which case you can type the URL in the Location field and Netscape will bring you directly to the page.

URLs appear complicated but are actually quite easy to decipher. The URL consists of several parts specifying the protocol, server, and path name of the item. Most begin with http://www or some variation. The URL for the Arizona State University home page is:

The protocol identifies a manner for interpreting computer information. For many Internet pages, the protocol is HTTP, for HyperText Transfer Protocol. Other protocols you will see are FTP (File Transfer Protocol), news (the protocol used by Usenet), and Gopher. The protocol is always followed by a colon. The server identifies the computer system that stores the information. The server is preceded with two forward slashes (//). The last part is the path name, which indicates where the information is located on the server. Each part of the path is preceded with a single forward slash (/).

The status bar at the bottom of the window contains buttons and text describing a page's location or the progress of a connection to a page when a transfer is in progress. It also displays a broken key symbol, which indicates whether the transfer of information exchange you are engaged in is secure or not. When the transmission is secure, the key is not broken. Most transfers of pages on Netscape are not secure. This means the information can be read and intercepted by others, making the transfer of confidential information, such as credit card numbers, susceptible to abuse. Netscape software allows you to make a transmission secure with a technology that makes the document an unreadable jumble during transit. This prevents an intermediary computer from accessing the document. Only the sending and receiving computers can read the document.

Selecting Links

Now that you are familiar with the parts of the Netscape window, you will explore your own home page information.

Point to any link on this page.

Notice that the URL for this link appears in the status bar. When the mouse pointer is positioned over highlighted words serving as a link to a page, the status bar shows the URL that will be used to bring the page to the screen.

Next you will select a hypertext link by clicking on it. Watch the information in the status bar while the next document is loaded.

Click on any hypertext link on your home page that indicates it will provide information about your school, such as admissions information, school libraries, or community information.

When you click on a link, the page that the link refers to is transferred from the server location to your location. The status indicator shows the number of kilobytes loaded of the total number while the page loads. In addition, a **progress bar** appears to show the progress of the current operation. The bar shows the percentage completed as a page loads. This information is important because many documents are very large and take a long time to load.

Depending upon what you selected, the content area may be displaying another page. Clicking on a link does not always bring a new page to the screen. Some links bring a different portion of the same document to the screen, saving you the trouble of scrolling to the area of interest. This is often the case when a page is a long document that contains a table of contents. Clicking on the table of contents link takes you to the beginning of that section of the document. Some links do not display a page at all, but may instead display a dialog box requesting more information.

If your content area displays a new page, the title bar and the location field show the new URL for this page.

Click on another link of your choice and observe the status bar while the page loads.

Information related to the topic you selected appears in the page in the content area.

Finally, select a third hypertext link.

You have selected three links that have taken you to different pages of information. Depending upon the content of the pages you have loaded, you have probably noticed that some pages take longer to load than others. If a page contains an image, it can take considerably longer to load because images are much larger in byte size than text. Usually, when people design pages, they take this factor into consideration, making the images small so the page loads faster. Images that are part of a page are called **inline images**, because they load automatically as part of the page.

To quickly return to your home page,

Click:

A hypertext link can also be images or icons with colored borders.

Your instructor may suggest a specific link.

If you want to stop loading a document, click the Stop button.

INTERNET

The default color for an
unfollowed link is blue and
for a followed link is purple.

Notice that the first link you selected appears in a different color. This indicates that you have viewed the page that this link will display. This link is called a **followed link**. It will remain a followed link for a set period of time, depending upon your program setup (the default is 30 days). If you have never clicked on a link before, it is an **unfollowed link**.

While you are using Netscape, the program maintains a history of the places you have visited. To see the history list,

Select: Go

Your screen should be similar to Figure 4-2.

FIGURE 4-2

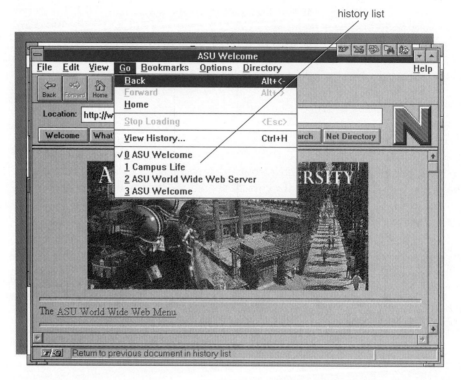

The lower portion of the menu displays a list of the page titles you have just selected while using Netscape. The most recent selection is at the top of the list. Clicking on any one of these will quickly return you to that location. As you make more selections, the older selections are removed from the history list.

Click on the third item in the list. The third page you viewed earlier is reloaded and displayed in the content area.

Click:

Just like Gopher, selecting hypertext links leads you from one location to another, and after many selections and possible diversions, you may finally reach your destination. If you are just exploring, this is fine. But what if you want to locate information about a specific topic? There are many methods you can use to search for information on the WWW. These include WWWW (World Wide Web Worm) and Web Crawler. Both search WWW titles for matching text, much like Veronica in Gopher. These tools are probably available as hypertext links from your school's pages. Otherwise, clicking the Net Search button will take you to a page that contains hypertext links to these tools.

Using Yahoo

Another tool that has been recently developed to help you locate information is called Yahoo. **Yahoo** is a database of Web pages containing, as of this writing, approximately 32,000 entries.

Because each home page is different, how you access Yahoo will vary. You may be able to select a link from one of your school's pages that will take you there. It is also currently easy to get to Yahoo by choosing the Net Directory button.

Select: the Yahoo link from your menu
or
Click: Net Directory
Click: Yahoo

After a few moments, the Yahoo home page is loaded.

Note: If you receive a message indicating you cannot connect to a site, it may be that the maximum number of users is accessing the location. Resubmit your request several times and you will probably get on. If not, skip to the section "Using the URL" on page IN123 and return to this section later.

Yahoo was developed at Stanford University by David File and Jerry Yang.

Things are always changing on the Net. Therefore, what was there when this book was written may not be there when you try this.

Look for the word Yahoo in a link, or your instructor may supply the sequence of links to select.

You can also access Yahoo by typing: http://www.yahoo.com/ in the Location field.

INTERNET

Your screen should be similar to Figure 4-3.

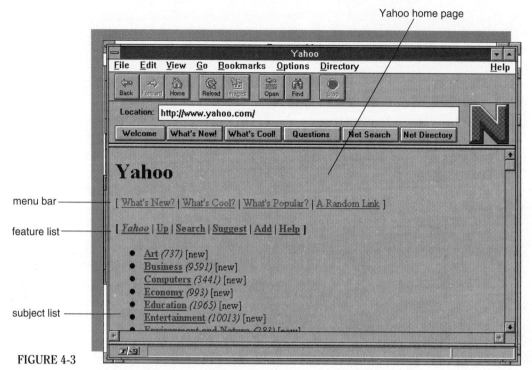

FIGURE 4-3

At the top of the Yahoo page is a hypertext menu bar and feature list. Selecting these links has the following effects:

Link	Effect
What's New?	Displays list of new database items added in the last five days
What's Cool?	Displays list of items authors think are "cool"
What's Popular?	Displays list of 50 most popular links used in last week
A Random Link	Randomly selects a link and loads it
Yahoo	Returns to Yahoo home page
Up	Moves up in hierarchy
Search	Displays a form for entry of search text
Suggest	Allows you to suggest improvements and comments on Yahoo
Add	Adds a URL to Yahoo list of hot topics
Help	Displays Yahoo Help information

Below the menu bar and features list, the Yahoo home page displays a hypertext subject list. Scroll the page to see the complete subject list.

Below the list, the number of total Yahoo entries is displayed. At the bottom of the page are other hypertext links to other very useful WWW directories.

You have heard that you can view paintings from the Louvre art museum in Paris using the WWW. To find art sources,

Click: Art

A listing of art categories appears.

Select: Museums

Your screen should be similar to Figure 4-4.

listing of art museums
in Yahoo's database

FIGURE 4-4

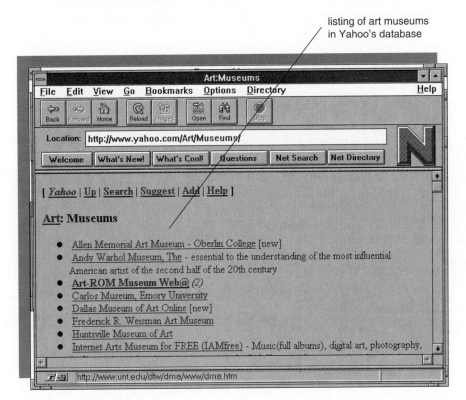

As you make selections, the hierarchy of topics is narrowed, much like using Gopher.

Select: Le Louvre

A list of WebMuseum sites is displayed. The WebMuseum is a database of information about the Louvre museum and Paris, and is available from several different sites. You need to choose the closest site to your school so the data access is faster. Select the site closest to your location.

The WebMuseum home page appears. The WebMuseum consists of two parts: an exhibit of art from Le Louvre and a tour of Paris. Scroll to the bottom of the page. To view images of famous paintings, from the General Exhibitions section,

Select: The Famous Paintings exhibition

Read about the exhibition and then select Impressionism from the Themes Index.
A list of artists is displayed. Select Mary Cassatt from the list.
Your screen should be similar to Figure 4-5.

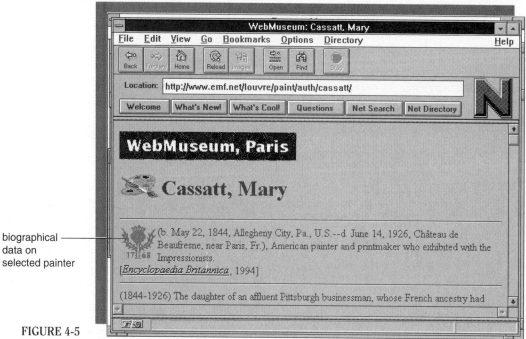

biographical data on selected painter

FIGURE 4-5

If you get an error message for the artist you selected, return to the beginning and try a different artist.

A brief biography of the artist appears.
Scroll the page to see **thumbnails** (miniature images) of several of the paintings created by this artist. To see a full-scale representation of one of the images, click on one of the thumbnails.

The graphic image occupies the entire content area. Scroll the window to view the entire image. This type of image is called an **external image**. External images on Netscape are stored as either GIF or JPEG file formats and are loaded into a separate window. The thumbnail is linked to the URL to access the image.

Next you want to return to the Yahoo directory to locate another topic.

You can also click [Back] to continue selecting from the WebMuseum page.

Choose: Go>Yahoo

This time, you want to read David Letterman's Top Ten list from the previous evening. Rather than trying to locate this list by making selections from narrowing topics, you will use the Search feature of Yahoo.

Click: Search

Your screen should be similar to Figure 4-6.

Yahoo search form

FIGURE 4-6

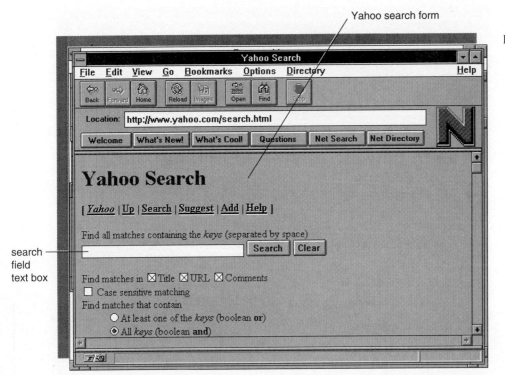

search
field
text box

The Yahoo Search form appears. Not only can you read information on pages in the WWW, you can interact by entering information on them. The Search form lets you enter text to search for and also lets you specify the scope of the search. To locate topics on David Letterman,

Click: search field text box

An insertion point appears. Now you can type the text you want Yahoo to locate.

Type: David Letterman
Select: Search

> Case sensitivity is off by default.

INTERNET

Your screen should be similar to Figure 4-7.

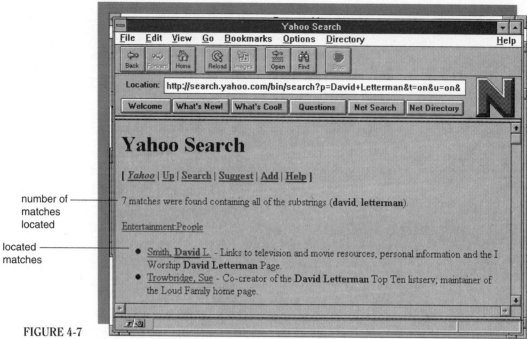

number of
matches
located

located
matches

FIGURE 4-7

After a few moments, Yahoo displays a list of all items in the database that match the search text.

Scroll the page and select the Late Show with David Letterman link. The Late Show home page is loaded.

Scroll the page to view the latest Top Ten list. A friend of yours who is a big Letterman fan has asked you to save a copy of this Top Ten list. To save a page,

Choose: File>Save as

In the dialog box, you need to specify the path and file name where you want to save the page. You can save the file on a floppy disk or on your hard drive. Select the directory that is appropriate for your situation.

The default file name lateshow.htm is displayed in the File Name text box. The file extension .htm indicates the file will contain the hypertext markup. To save it as a text file, in the File Name text box,

Type: lateshow.txt
Choose: OK

If you receive a message indicating there is a machine overload, click ⬅ and resubmit your search. It may take several tries before your search is processed.

You may need to scroll the page to see this hypertext.

The shortcut for this command is Ctrl + S.

The page is downloaded to the location you specified and can be accessed like any text file.

To return to your home page,

Click:

Using the URL

Another area of interest that the Web is especially suited to is travel information. This is because, in addition to text, the Web can display photographs and maps, making it popular with travel providers.

One of best places to look for travel information is the Virtual Tourist project, a directory of travel-related Web resources located at the address http://wings.buffalo.edu/world. To go directly to this location, you can type the URL in the Location field. Typing the URL will take you instantly to the location. Many books, news articles, and discussion groups will provide URLs for you, saving you a lot of search time.

Click: Location field

An insertion point appears. Highlight the existing text. To enter a new location,

Drag to highlight text.

Type: http://wings.buffalo.edu/world/vt2/
Press: ←Enter

Your screen should be similar to Figure 4-8.

FIGURE 4-8

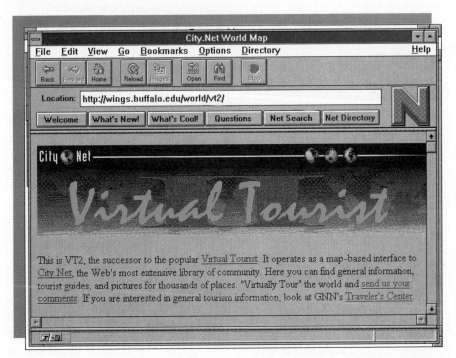

INTERNET

The Virtual Tourist home page is loaded. Scroll the page until the map of the world is displayed.

You are planning a trip to England and are interested in tourist information about this area. From the world map, to access information on European countries,

Click: Europe

Another page is loaded. It includes a map of the European countries.

Click: United Kingdom

This page provides links to different areas within the United Kingdom. To find information on England,

Click: England

To find information on London,

Click: London

The new page displays links for city information and transportation. You would like to use the city guide link.

Click: The London Guide

Your screen should be similar to Figure 4-9.

FIGURE 4-9

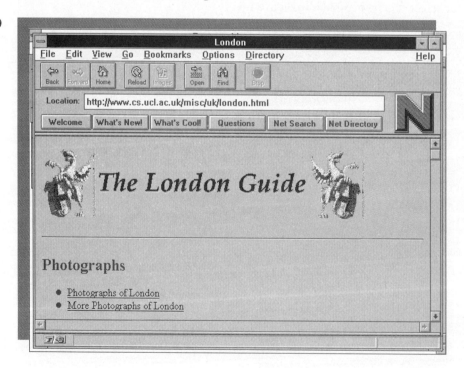

You decide you may want to spend time at this location. You can create bookmarks to WWW pages using the Add Bookmark option on the Bookmarks menu. Bookmarks are saved on lists and can be accessed using the View Bookmarks option on the Bookmarks menu. This is similar to Bookmarks in Gopher. Add the current location to the bookmark list.

Make a selection from this page and browse through additional links to read information about restaurants and hotels, museums, play reviews, and to view photographs of the area you have selected. When you are done, return to your home page.

Reading Newsgroups Using Netscape

Note: If your school's setup does not allow access to newsgroups through Netscape, skip this section.

Using Netscape, you can also read and write to newsgroups. To display the page of subscribed newsgroups,

Select: Directory>Go To Newsgroups
or
Click: Newsgroups

Your screen should be similar to Figure 4-10.

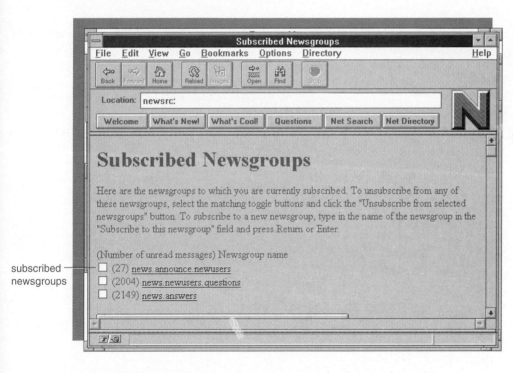

subscribed newsgroups

> If a message appears indicating that your RC file is not created, choose OK so that Netscape can create it for you.

FIGURE 4-10

The Newsgroup page displays the current list of subscribed newsgroups.

If you are not subscribed to any newsgroups, follow the instructions on the page to subscribe to the news.announce.newusers newsgroup.

To read a newsgroup, click on a newsgroup of your choice.

Your screen should be similar to Figure 4-11.

newsgroup
buttons

articles in
selected
newsgroup

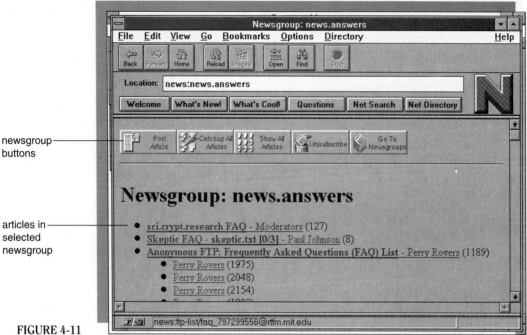

FIGURE 4-11

A page that lists the articles in the newsgroup you selected appears. The newsgroup buttons allow you to post a new article, mark all articles as read, show all articles or only new articles, subscribe to the newsgroup, and go to the list of subscribed newsgroups. The same buttons are displayed at the end of the listing of articles.

Scroll the page to view additional articles. Depending on the list you are viewing, you may see that the listing page is in outline format. New topics are preceded with large bullets, and responses to a topic are indented one level in from the original posting. A new response is indented another level. This clearly identifies the threads of topics in the newsgroup.

Click on any article to read it.

Your screen should be similar to Figure 4-12.

buttons —

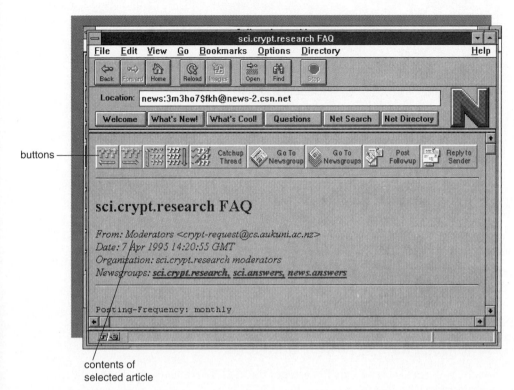

contents of
selected article

FIGURE 4-12

The page displays the contents of the selected article. The buttons at the top of the page are used to navigate threads, mark a thread as read, go to the article list, go to the list of subscribed newsgroups, and post a reply to the article or the article's author. They are also displayed at the end of the article.

Scroll the page to read the article. If the topic you selected has a thread, click ▦ to read next posting.

When you are done, to return to the list of subscribed newsgroups,

Click: Go To Newsgroups

To subscribe to more newsgroups, you could type the newsgroup address in the Subscribe Field text box. Alternatively, you can view a list of all newsgroups, and select from the list. To do this,

> You may need to scroll the window to see the text box.

Click: View all newsgroups

In response to the informational message regarding loading the newsgroup list,

Select: OK

After a few moments, the newsgroup categories list is displayed.

Select a category and then a newsgroup of your choice. The newsgroup article list is displayed. To subscribe to it,

Click:

The newsgroup is added to your list of newsgroup subscriptions.

Select the newsgroup you just subscribed to and read any articles that may be of interest to you. Use the button to return to the articles list.

Articles you have read appear in purple, just as any other followed link. To return to the newgroup subscription page,

Click:

To unsubscribe to a newsgroup, simply mark the newsgroup by clicking on the box and then click the [Unsubscribe from selected newsgroups] button.

Click: [Home]

Sending E-Mail Through Netscape

Finally, you can also send e-mail messages through Netscape. At this time, however, you cannot receive incoming e-mail.

To send e-mail,

Select: File>Mail Document

> The shortcut for this command is Ctrl + M.

Your screen should be similar to Figure 4-13.

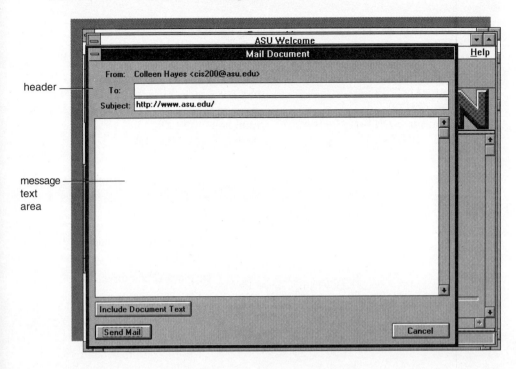

FIGURE 4-13

The Mail Document dialog box is displayed. It contains areas for you to enter the e-mail address of the recipient, the subject, and a message. One convenient feature is the ability to insert the text of the current page you are viewing in the message area or as an attachment as a separate file to be sent with your e-mail message. This is done using the Include Document Text button. The Send button transmits your e-mail message.

Since you are already familiar with this process, you will not send a message. To return to your home page,

Choose: Cancel

To exit Netscape,

Select: File>Exit
or
Double-click: control-menu box

You are returned to Windows Program Manager.

If a message appears instructing you to enter your e-mail address, follow the instructions by adding your name and address in the Mail and Proxies window, then repeat the File>Mail Document command.

INTERNET

Key Terms

World Wide Web (IN111)	URL (IN114)
page (IN111)	progress bar (IN115)
hypertext link (IN111)	inline image (IN115)
browser (IN111)	followed link (IN116)
Netscape (IN112)	unfollowed link (IN116)
home page (IN113)	Yahoo (IN117)
Directory button (IN114)	thumbnail (IN120)
content area (IN114)	external image (IN120)

Command Summary

Command	Shortcut Key	Action
Go		Displays history of pages viewed
Go>**Y**ahoo		Displays Yahoo directory
Bookmarks>**A**dd Bookmark	Ctrl + A	Adds current document to bookmark list
Bookmarks>View **B**ookmarks	Ctrl + B	Displays bookmark list
File>**S**ave as	Ctrl + S	Saves file with new name
Directory>**G**o To Newsgroups		Displays page of newsgroups subscribed to
File>**M**ail Document	Ctrl + M	Sends e-mail message

Matching

1. WWW _____ **a.** search directory for WWW

2. hypertext _____ **b.** World Wide Web browser

3. home page _____ **c.** highlighted or underlined text or graphic that moves you to related document

4. browser _____ **d.** returns to home page

5. Netscape _____ **e.** World Wide Web

6. Yahoo _____ **f.** interface to WWW

7. pages _____ **g.** WWW address

8. URL _____ **h.** text link to another page or file

9. hypertext links _____ **i.** screens containing text and graphics

10. _____ **j.** page loaded automatically when program is opened

Short-Answer Questions

1. What is the World Wide Web?
2. What is the difference between WWW and Gopher?
3. What is Netscape?
4. What is a hypertext document?
5. What does HTML stand for?
6. How are the hypertext links identified in Netscape?
7. How can you search for information on the WWW?
8. What is a URL? Explain the parts of a URL.
9. How do you join a newsgroup on WWW?
10. What is a limitation of e-mail through Netscape?

Practice Exercises

1. Using Netscape, locate a picture of the Mona Lisa. Write down the URL for the picture location. Download the graphic file.

2. Would you like to talk to the astronauts in space? Try the address: http://astros.msfc.nasa.gov/. Want a guided tour of the Grand Canyon? Try the address: http://www.kbt.com/gc/gc_home.html.

3. Using Yahoo, search on San Francisco and locate the Reservations home page. This home page allows you to locate hotel rooms in the city by price, location, type of hotel, and so on. You can also view photographs of hotel lobbies and rooms. Use the home page to check availability. After checking out three hotels, which one would you recommend staying in and why?

4. PCTravel is a Web site that accesses the Apollo Reservation System. You need to use a credit card to establish a free account with PCTravel and then you can check schedules, fares, and availability on more than 500 airlines. The system automatically displays the lowest available fare for an itinerary and can be used to book reservations and send tickets to the user. If you have a credit card, establish an account and check prices for a trip you would like to take.

5. Another popular WWW site is TVNet. It is home to information about networks and stations, and displays listings of programs on TV that night and pointers to TV information across the Internet. TVNet's Ultimate TV List is an organized list of Internet resources on TV shows. It can guide you to information, discussions, and so on about 163 shows. See what you can find when you use the address: http://www.tvnet.com/TVnet.html.

6. You are preparing a paper for a course in your field of study.

  a. Use Netscape to locate three text files that contain information on the topic of your paper.

  b. Write down the text file names as they appear in the menu and write a brief summary of the information in the text files. (Remember, you can download the files to your disk. Check the size of the file before you download it to ensure that you have enough disk space.)

7. Several newspapers around the world now offer on-line editions on the World Wide Web. Typically, this includes not only copies of current news and sports stories, but features and, increasingly, advertisements. Use the following URLs to read current news stories.

Address	Newspaper
http://www.nando.net	Charlotte News and Observer (North Carolina)
http://www.sjmercury.com	San Jose Mercury News (California)
http://www.telegraph.co.uk.	The London Telegraph's Electronic Telegraph (United Kingdom)
http://www.timeinc.com	Time magazine

Additional WWW Addresses

Topic	Address	Description
Boston	http://www.std.com/ne/boston.html	An on-line guide to the city from restaurant and movie listings to car-repair recommendations and neighborhood profiles.
California	http://www.research.digital.com/src/virtual-tourist/california.html	This is your basic tourist-info center. It offers everything from traffic and road-condition reports to maps and pictures of tourist attractions.
China	http://www.ihep.ac.cn:3000/ihep.html	This is the People's Republic of China's first Internet connection, run by the Institute for High Energy Physics in Beijing, provid-ing everything from e-mail addresses of Chinese scientists to information on Chinese regions and a directory of foreign companies in Beijing.
Computer games	http://wcl-rs.bham.ac.uk/gamesdomain	The Games Domain is the place to go for information on dozens of computer games. Resources include hints for specific games and an on-line games magazine.
Congress	http://www.econet.apc.org/lcv/scorecard.html	See how your local congressperson is ranked by the League of Conservation Voters.
Congressional bills	http://thomas.loc.gov	The Library of Congress's Thomas (as in Thomas Jefferson) service lets you look up pending bills by keyword and read the *Congressional Record* (back to January, 1994).
Dinosaurs	http://www.hcc.hawaii.edu/dinos/dinos1.html	Look here for images of dinosaur skeletons.
Disney	http://bvp.wdp.com/bvpm/	The Buena Vista Pictures Web server has information and photos of current Disney and Buena Vista Pictures movies —even some QuickTime loops for Macintosh owners. (Warning: these are large files.)
Dublin bars	http://www.dsg.cs.tcd.ie/dsg_people/czimmerm/pubs.html	This is the definitive review of Dublin's watering holes.

(continued)

INTERNET

Additional WWW Addresses

Topic	Address	Description
Government information	http://www.fedworld.gov	FedWorld is a gateway to dozens of federal information services in the U.S., some free, some requiring a fee to use.
Golf	http://www.tr_riscs.panam.edu/golf/19thhole.html	Look for all sorts of golf information.
Legal information	http://www.law.cornell.edu/lii.table.html	Cornell University's Legal Information Institute provides a variety of law-related documents, including information on specific legal issues and copies of U.S. Supreme Court decisions.
Movies	http://www.cm.cf.ac.uk/movies/moviewquery.html	You can search for filmographies of particular actors and directors here.
Music	http://www.music.indiana.edu/misc/music_resources.html	This resource at Indiana University will help you find Web sites devoted to virtually every type of music and band.
White House	http://www.whitehouse.gov	Tours and more of the White House.
Wine	http://augustus.csscr.washington.edu/personal/bigstar-mosaic/wine.html	Look for information about the grape beverage here. Besides links to other Internet resources, it also lets you leave tasting notes for other enthusiasts, and provides information on wineries in Washington state.

The Internet

Glossary of Key Terms

Address: A means of uniquely identifying users and locations on a network.

Address book: In Pine, a collection of names and e-mail addresses.

Archive: To save e-mail messages.

Article: Message posted to a newsgroup.

Attachment: A text or graphic file that is attached to an e-mail message.

Bitnet: E-mail and file-sharing network used by academic and research institutions.

Body: The message text area of an e-mail message.

Bookmark: A means of marking your location in gopherspace or the WWW.

Browser: A program used to display text and images, to access FTP sites, and to provide an interface to the Internet and WWW documents.

Client: A program on your computer that interprets the user's keystrokes and commands and connects via a network to a server program.

Content area: The area of the Netscape window that displays the pages of information.

Context-sensitive: A Help system that provides information directly related to the screen you are currently viewing.

Cursor: A blinking box that shows where each character you type will appear.

Directory buttons: On a browser, buttons that access pages with information that help you browse the Internet.

Domain Name System (DNS): The e-mail addressing system used on the Internet.

Download: To copy a file to your computer from a remote site.

E-mail: Electronic mail. A message that is sent between users along network channels.

Emoticon: Picture of smiling or winking face used to add tone to e-mail.

Eudora: A Windows-based e-mail program that is used to send and reply to e-mail messages.

External image: In Netscape, a graphic that appears in a window by itself.

FAQ: A message that includes answers to Frequently Asked Questions.

Flame: Ranting and raving e-mail message.

Folder: In Pine, an area that is used to store messages.

Followed link: A link that you have clicked on.

Forward: To pass a message along to another e-mail address.

FTP: File Transfer Protocol; a system for transferring files across the Internet.

Gateway: A computer that translates e-mail messages from the protocol used on one network to that used on another network.

GIF: Graphic Interchange Format; file extension indicating that the file contains a graphic image.

Global address book: In Pine, a group of names and e-mail addresses that identify users or a computer at a specific location.

Gopher: A program for retrieving information on the Internet.

Gopherspace: All the information that is available on all the Gopher servers on the Internet.

Header: Contains the addressing information required to send an e-mail message.

Hierarchy: The different categories of newsgroups.

History list: A list of locations you have accessed during your current session while using Gopher.

Home Gopher menu: The opening Gopher screen, which displays the directory menu for the Gopher server at the host site.

Home page: The first page loaded by a World Wide Web browser.

Hypertext link: A highlighted keyword or graphic image that when clicked on with the mouse links users to a related document.

Inline image: An image that is part of a page.

List address: E-mail address used to participate in mailing list discussions.

Listserv: The Bitnet program used to send e-mail to and from a list of particular subscribers. Usually organized around a discussion topic.

Listserv address: E-mail address used to subscribe to a mailing list.

Mailbox: In Eudora, an area that is used to store messages.

Mailing list: Program that sends e-mail to and from a particular list of subscribers.

Moderated newsgroup: Newsgroup where postings are reviewed by a moderator before being forwarded to the entire group.

Netiquette: The standard rules of courteous electronic communications.

Netscape: A hypertext browser program designed to locate information on the WWW.

Newsgroup: Electronic forums in Usenet. Each newsgroup has a fairly narrow and defined subject area.

Newsgroup site: A computer that participates in the network news system.

Newsreader: A program designed to help users read newsgroup messages.

Nickname: A complete or shortened name used to identify a recipient of e-mail.

Page: A single screen on the World Wide Web.

Pine: A menu-based e-mail program that makes sending and replying to mail easy.

Post: To send a message to a mailing list.

Progress bar: A bar that shows the status of a transmission.

Protocol: The rules that control how software and hardware communicate on a network.

Recipient list: In Eudora, a collection of names and e-mail addresses.

Root Gopher menu: The opening Gopher screen, which displays the directory menu for the Gopher server at the host site.

Server: A program that holds information, providing it to clients on request.

Shout: To type a message in all uppercase characters.

Signature line: A personalized identification that is added to the end of the body of a message.

Smiley: Picture of smiling or winking face used to add tone to e-mail.

Spell checker: Program used to check the spelling of a document.

Status bar: A line at the bottom of the Netscape window that displays information about the number of bytes received.

Status indicator: In Pine, the notations on the message header line that indicate the status of a message, such as D for delete.

Status line: In Pine, the top line of the screen, which displays information about the program status.

Store-and-forward: A system of mail forwarding that routinely holds messages for later batch sending.

Subscription address: E-mail address used to subscribe to a mailing list.

Telnet: The standard program for logging onto computers on the Internet.

Thread: A conversation in a newsgroup, with articles and responses grouped together in order.

Thumbnail: Miniature image displayed on a page.

Trumpet: A newsreader program that lets you subscribe to and read newsgroup messages.

Unfollowed link: A link that you have never clicked on or followed.

Unmoderated newsgroup: Newsgroup where postings are not reviewed by a moderator before being forwarded to the entire group.

Upload: To send a file to another computer.

URL: Uniform Resource Locator; provides location information that is used to navigate through the Internet to access a particular page.

Usenet: The network of newsgroups on the Internet.

Veronica: A search tool that assists in finding information in gopherspace.

White pages: A database commonly available through Gopher in which you can search for an e-mail address.

World Wide Web (WWW): A collection of pages and sites from which you can access information.

Yahoo: A directory search program used on the WWW to help quickly locate information.

INTERNET

NOTES